LIFE
GOES TO
WAR

A Picture History of World War II

A WALLABY BOOK

PUBLISHED BY SIMON & SCHUSTER, NEW YORK

TIME-LIFE TELEVISION BOOKS

Editor: Eleanor Graves
Associate Editor: Charles Osborne

LIFE GOES TO WAR

Editor: DAVID E. SCHERMAN
Art Director: ROBERT CLIVE
Staff Writers: James A. Randall,
Ruth Kelton
Researchers: Joyce Pelto (Chief),
Ann Guerin, Mary Carroll Marden,
Carolyn Tasker
Assistant Art Director: Lou Valentino
Copy Chief: Eleanor Van Bellingham
Editorial Production: Mary Jane Hodges,
Sarah Magee, Antoinette Mellilo,
Connie Nicholson

Frank K. Kappler, who has written special
material for this volume, including the
chapter introductions, saw action in World
War II in the Aleutians and in Italy as a
sergeant in the Tenth Mountain Division.
He was for many years a LIFE writer and
editor and is currently a writer for *People*.

Valuable assistance was given by the
Time Inc. Picture Collection,
Doris O'Neil (Chief), Jorge Gonzalez,
Joseph E. Schilling; by George J. Karas
(Chief), Herbert Orth,
Peter Christopoulos, Renate Haarhoff,
Len Shay and Shirley Terry of the
Time Inc. Photographic Laboratory;
by Lillian Owens and Diana D. Franklin
of the Time Inc. Archives.

Published by Wallaby Books,
A Simon & Schuster Division of
Gulf & Western Corporation,
Simon & Schuster Building,
1230 Avenue of the Americas,
New York, New York 10020
WALLABY and colophon are trademarks
of Simon & Schuster
Reprinted by arrangement with Little, Brown & Co. in
association with Time-Life Films, Inc.
For information address Little, Brown & Co.,
34 Beacon Street, Boston, MA 02106

10   9   8   7   6   5   4

Manufactured in the United States of America

Library of Congress Cataloging in Publication Data

Main entry under title:

Life goes to war.

   Reprint of the ed. published by Little, Brown,
Boston.
   "A Wallaby book."
   Includes index.
   1. World War, 1939-1945—Pictorial works.
I. Life (Chicago)
[D743.2.L483   1981]   940.53′022′2   80-26309
ISBN 0-671-79077-3

CONTENTS

Carl Mydans after internment in Shanghai

Shelley Smith Mydans, a Bible under her arm, with a Filipino troop returning from a field Mass in 1941

Margaret Bourke-White and Red Army soldiers

William Vandivert and Theodore H. White in Sinkiang, China

Bob Landry in Sicily, just after invasion

Eliot Elisofon and old friend Patton in Africa

George Rodger behind a bullet-shattered window in Burma

The Longest Story

It was the longest story LIFE ever told. It began in 1936 on the blood-stained barricades of Madrid and Barcelona and the wind-swept plains above Peking, and it ended, nine years later, on the deck of a battleship in Tokyo Bay.

This is a book about that story—the Second World War—and how it was reported by the combat journalists, photographers and reporters of LIFE. It is not intended to be a comprehensive analysis of that war. Rather, it is intended as a retrospective report, composed entirely from the wartime pages of LIFE, on the battlefronts of that conflict. And, since this was a truly total war, in which civilians were as often the heroes and victims as the combatants, it is a report from the home fronts too.

LIFE, which existed from 1936 to 1972, was a picture magazine, the first and perhaps the last of its kind. Its chief concern was visual; during World War II, it de-

ployed more photographers and artists than all the newspapers of the United States combined. All of them, at one time or another, were in grave danger, since it was quite impossible to photograph frontline action from a rear-echelon command post. As war photographer Robert Capa once put it: "If your pictures are no good, you aren't close enough." Most of the LIFE people shown above and overleaf found themselves with the advancing troops, and—occasionally—even in front of them looking back. The result was inevitable: five photographers were wounded in action, two sailed aboard ships that were torpedoed, two were shot down and a dozen found themselves overboard during naval operations.

As LIFE's grateful editors pointed out in 1945, the miracle was not that these emissaries brought home such a complete record of the war, but that they brought themselves home as well. No photographer was killed, although four brave LIFE men died in subsequent wars. But the photographers had no corner on bravery. Reporters John Hersey, Bob Sherrod, Bill Walton, Will

George Silk in his Anzac headgear

Charles Wertenbaker in London

Robert Capa in paratroop gear

John Phillips en route to Rome

J. R. Eyerman commuting between ships

David Fredenthal on an airstrip

Leonard McCombe covering German DPs

Myron Davis after the attack on Lae

Ralph Morse at surrender table

Lang and a score of other *Time* and LIFE men were in continual hazard. Jack Belden was badly wounded at Salerno. Correspondents Melville Jacoby and Bill Chickering were killed in the Far East. LIFE reporter Andrew Heiskell, now Chairman of the Board of Time Inc., was almost shot as a German parachutist by trigger-happy French civilians during the collapse of Paris in 1940. (Photographer Carl Mydans, who was with him, and spoke no French, saved the day by shouting, "Translate, Heiskell! For God's sake, translate!")

The peculiar quality of the wartime journalist's bravery is its element of choice. As usual, Bob Capa, who despite an almost impenetrable Hungarian accent was easily the most articulate of the press corps, put it most succinctly: "I would say that the war correspondent gets more drinks, more girls, better pay and greater freedom than the soldiers, but having the freedom to choose his spot and being allowed to be a coward and not be executed

for it is his torture. The war correspondent has his stake—his life—in his own hands and he can put it on this horse or that horse, or he can put it back in his pocket at the very last minute." Myron Davis, recalling the South Pacific attack at Lae and Salamaua, agrees that "nobody could *order* a reporter to be in a landing barge. At first Bob Cromie [of the Chicago Tribune] and I were not wanted by the men in the barge because we were strangers. When they found we were civilians, and there by choice, we became sort of heroes. 'You mean you don't *have* to be here—you could be fat-catting in Sydney if you wanted?' When we said we could, they said, 'You must be crazy.' "

Capa recalled a similar observation shouted at him by a paratrooper as the latter dropped out the waist exit of a C-47 over Sicily: "I don't like your job—it's too dangerous!" And hours before he was wounded at Okinawa, where he was covering infantryman Terry Moore of the Seventh Division, Eugene Smith had the same thought: "I envied Terry Moore. He had been *ordered* in. Even

Ed Clark in Paris after V-E Day

Peter Stackpole amidst Saipan ruins

War Artist Tom Lea in the Pacific

Gene Smith on an aerial assignment

Mel Jacoby writing at Corregidor

David Scherman in a Breton apple orchard

Dmitri Kessel on a Middle East assignment

Ralph Crane covering the U.S. Southwest

Frank Scherschel on Atlantic convoy duty

now I could drop out. He had only fear. I had fear and the recurrent thought, 'What am I doing here?'"

In that context, a variety of motivations kept the LIFE people going: curiosity, pride, professionalism, sometimes plain anger. It was certainly some form of justifiable anger that inspired Fritz Goro and Otto Hagel, both German-born Americans, to expose the destructive activities of some of their compatriots by covertly joining them at great personal risk. Goro joined the Canadian Nazis, who virtually disbanded after his story on them appeared in LIFE, and Hagel signed on with the German-American Bund in the U.S. *(page 34)*. The acceptance of danger seemed courageous in Goro's case. Fritz is a shy, scholarly scientist more at home photographing the mysteries of nuclear fission—as he did prophetically *(page 300)*—than posing as a Nazi.

Sheer professionalism was often the spur. Frank Scherschel, a lifelong news photographer and onetime pilot, considered danger as much a part of his normal business as flashbulbs. He admits to having been scared stiff, though too busy to do anything about it, while being shot at on North Atlantic convoy duty or en route to Stuttgart in a B-17. But he swears that he was not at all. frightened when German snipers opened fire on him, and everyone else, in Paris on Liberation Day: "It was just like covering a strike in Milwaukee." The late Paul Dorsey, a laconic Los Angeles policeman turned news photographer, scoffed at any motivation other than plain business. "We're not heroes, or adventurers, or sensitive artists," he used to insist. "We're tradesmen—plumbers, bricklayers!" In his case, that prosaic dictum was simply false modesty. After brilliantly covering the China war from Japan's side long before Pearl Harbor, he joined the Marines and suffered all the rest of his life from malaria contracted in the South Pacific.

LIFE's two most indestructible photographers were no strangers to war decades before the invasion of Poland. Alfred Eisenstaedt, whom many consider the father of modern photojournalism, was wounded as a German corporal in World War I. He recovered sufficiently to immortalize the first meeting of Hitler and Mussolini *(page 22)*, cover the latter's conquest of Ethiopia, and finally establish himself firmly enough near Times Square, New York City, to shoot the last page of this book there on V-J Day, 1945. Dmitri Kessel, as a war photographer covering the Russian Revolution in 1918, had his first camera broken over his head by a Red Army officer, was drafted into the Ukrainian Army, was captured and wound up in the Red cavalry. A civilian by World War II, he joined LIFE's staff and was for years thereafter constantly under fire.

Compassion moved many correspondents, particularly LIFE's war artists Tom Lea, Fletcher Martin, Bernard Perlin and the late David Fredenthal. A rare humanity flowed into their paintings of wartime suffering in Pacific jungles, the African desert and the caves of guerrillas. Photographer Ralph Morse, whose odyssey of a wounded GI's medical treatment is a World War II classic, is no stranger to compassion, nor to wounded GIs. In the waters off Guadalcanal in 1942 he supported a life-jacketless shipmate from the sunken cruiser *Vincennes* for six hours. In Normandy, two years later, he was seen (and painted by a combat artist) carrying wounded soldiers out of the wreckage of St. Lô.

"My God, it's Carl Mydans!" This unbelieving cry arose among the emaciated inmates of a Manila prison camp after a special MacArthur task force had raced through the countryside to rescue them from last-minute annihilation by the Japanese. The LIFE photographer with his wife, reporter Shelley Smith, had once been fellow prisoners; they had been repatriated and he was now returning, MacArthur-like, to help with the rescue operation. Energetic and indefatigably cheerful, Mydans has covered war globally (China, Finland, Singapore, Italy, Japan and Korea) since LIFE's inception. He has combined the essential qualities of a good war journalist—compassion, curiosity, professionalism—and most valuable of all, a sense of humor.

War is a tragedy at best, but without its comic moments it can be unbearably grim. Johnny Florea, who reported the tragic massacre at the Battle of the Bulge, invented a mythical German town called Unterstitzen-on-the-Bleiweis. "When do we take Unterstitzen, General?" he would ask at press conferences. "Within a week at most," was the usual reply. Bernard Hoffman is a quiet practical joker who was trapped behind enemy lines in Burma, having chuted in with Merrill's Marauders. He recalls a delicious meal he once scrounged. When he asked his hosts what it was, they smiled and pointed to four uncooked dogs' heads. George Rodger is a courtly Englishman who spent months and traveled 75,000 miles on a LIFE assignment in 1942 that took him to every continent but Australia, only to produce his greatest picture *(page 263)* in an instant near the end of the war in his home base, London. George Silk is a brash and talented New Zealander to whom the editors in 1945 gave carte blanche to "carpetbag" his angry colleagues on whatever European fronts he chose. It turned out to be a wise decision, since he usually managed to be where the good pictures were to be made. But even he was not immune to the tension of combat. Under German shellfire in Italy, he once tried frantically for five minutes to load a new roll of film in his camera; then LIFE's Will Lang, in the same foxhole, quietly pointed out that the "film" was a roll of Life Savers.

Those five minutes, possibly the longest in Silk's career, were only a moment in LIFE's longest story. That story—at least in a legend dear to the editors—got poignantly reassuring feedback from a group of unexpected readers some time after it had officially ended. On November 5, 1945, the legend runs, 22 Japanese emerged from a jungle on Guam and surrendered to a passing GI truckdriver, handing him a copy of LIFE's September 17 issue, which covered V-E Day. Attached to it was this note in clear, if painful, English: "We had been lived in this jangle from last year but we know by this book the War end."

DAVID E. SCHERMAN

A photographer for LIFE in April 1941, when he was sunk at sea by a German raider, Scherman survived to cover the remainder of World War II in England, France and Germany. A LIFE editor for many years, he is also the editor of Best of LIFE *and* LIFE Goes to the Movies.

George Strock in formal attire

John Florea on a half-track in Germany in 1945

Bernard Hoffman in the jungle

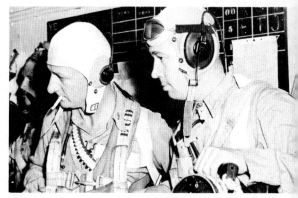

Bob Sherrod and Marine photographer in the Pacific

William Walton on a convoy

Will Lang and an antiaircraft officer in Italy

William Shrout in Navy goggles

Paul Dorsey arguing in Tokyo

Alfred Eisenstaedt in Northern Japan with the Ainu

1936

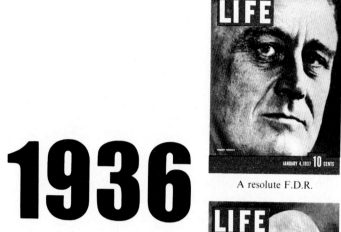

A resolute F.D.R.

An experimental parachute

Betrayed Czech defender

Hirohito's general

Warlike Japanese boy

American airman

1939

Supermen of Japan

Graduating midshipmen

Hungarian guard

Memento of another War

Teen-age Chinese soldier

Prewar military bride

I. OVERTURE

The curtain rises with war in Europe and Asia

"Let him who desires peace prepare for war." In the early 1930s, Americans and the peoples of Europe were in no mood to listen to the conventional wisdom of the Roman military writer Vegetius. They were coping with the early stages of the Great Depression. And while most were disillusioned after the 1914–1918 War to End War, it was easy to ignore signs that the seeds of a second world war were being sown. Germany had begun incubating military pilots by teaching boys to fly gliders. Two other nations, Mussolini's Fascist Italy and militarist Japan, were flexing their muscles and eyeing their neighbors' territory. The League of Nations, without the U.S., seemed increasingly incapable of agreeing on the rules for world order.

Japan's rape of Manchuria in 1931, Hitler's rise to power in 1933, his prompt rebuilding of the German Army, and Mussolini's 1935–1939 conquest of Ethiopia may have stirred indignation. But the events made no noticeable dent in the Western democracies' isolationist sense that all those places were far away. In 1936, Italy and Nazi Germany rushed to the aid of Francisco Franco's Falangist revolt against the Spanish Republic and turned it into a dress rehearsal for what was to come. Then the U.S.S.R. riposted by coming to the aid of the Republic. But the response of most Americans reflected the words of novelist Sinclair Lewis' ironic title, *It Can't Happen Here.*

LIFE was launched the same year the Spanish Civil War began. The editors of the new magazine pledged "to see the world, to eyewitness great events." They also rightly sensed the need to picture an America that its readers would quickly recognize. For some time LIFE looked inward. Early issues were full of Fred Astaire, Henry Ford, Shirley Temple and the Dionne quintuplets. Pages featured picture essays on subjects like college life at Vassar, a documentary movie on *The Birth of a Baby*, Hollywood high jinks and fashions. It published outstanding news photographs, from the explosion of the airship *Hindenburg* in Lakehurst, New Jersey, to the impact of a heckler's egg on socialist Norman Thomas' forehead at a Jersey City rally.

Yet despite its preoccupation with the scene at home, the magazine was well aware of storm signals from abroad. It cast a sharp eye on foreign events and personalities. In the first few weeks of its existence, for example, LIFE published picture biographies of Stalin, Hitler and Mussolini. It sent Margaret Bourke-White to Europe to photograph the dominoes that were to to fall in Hitler's path. Other journalists with picture scoops gravitated to the picture magazine. One was a footloose Hungarian, Robert Capa, just out of his teens, whose photographs of the internecine fighting in Spain fairly leaped out of LIFE's pages.

Another journalist with a sense of history and mission was young Edgar Snow, who befriended and photographed an unknown young Communist firebrand in China with a $250,000 price on his head as a bandit. The first victim of what was to become the Axis, China was of particular interest to LIFE since its founder, Henry R. Luce, had been born and reared there. Luce was a strong, early supporter of Chiang Kai-shek, the soldier who, as head of the republic founded in 1911 by Sun Yat-Sen, had striven with such success to unify China.

In the neutralist years before 1939, LIFE took a strong stand. From the beginning, it made no bones about its preference for the Republican cause in Spain, and repeatedly stated its aversion to dictatorship and militarism. Eager to bolster America's defense against these dangers, LIFE visited still-sleepy Army bases and Navy installations as well as West Point and Annapolis, making friends of young officers whom readers were to meet later as generals and admirals. The editors had their differences with President Franklin Roosevelt in the domestic area, but they were behind him on the need to awaken America to the pervasiveness of the Axis threat.

History has vindicated the magazine on that basic point—and on many of the details as well. Now and then its crystal ball clouded—when it unhesitatingly doubted Russia's willingness to fight and touted France's ability to do so. But as it turned out, there was nothing clouded in the vision evoked by the lines in its issue dated August 28, 1939: "Last week in Europe ten million men slept on their rifles, ready for the possible outbreak of a Second World War."

Spain: Faces of War

In 1936, when LIFE was born, the nation was suffering through a depression. But LIFE's editors saw the beginning of an even greater time of troubles in Europe, where a bloody Spanish civil war raged between Rebel army troops and Loyalist supporters of the Republican government. With the growing Fascist powers, Italy and Germany, supporting the insurgents, the conflict was the curtain-raiser to an awesome nine-year spectacle of violence and a journalistic challenge to America's first picture magazine.

While Germany and Italy tried their new weapons in Spain, the magazine experimented with a new way of reporting war—shown here as moving closeups of citizen-soldiers and embattled women reacting to war's totality.

Like war itself, combat photography had undergone a fundamental change. It was no longer the time-consuming record made by Mathew Brady posing troops for his cumbersome field camera. Now it was an image often preserved by a rapid-fire 35mm camera in the hands of one of LIFE's steadily growing worldwide staff.

A grizzled militiaman, cigarette clamped in his mouth, is a figure of defiance. An article on the training of such Republican citizen-volunteers noted their transformation from a rabble into a "real Army"—though in fact they never approached the professionalism of their foes.

A broad grin lights up the face of a Madrid militiaman as a government fighter plane attacks a Rebel aircraft. The photograph was included in LIFE's first picture-story by famed war photographer Robert Capa.

This somber Republican standard-▶ bearer appeared in LIFE's first issue, which reported on Republican Spain's women volunteers: "Pictures of pretty girls in arms have given the Spanish Government its most successful propaganda. But in gruesome fact the trenches around Madrid have been piled high with the bodies of brave, if foolish, Spanish women killed in action."

"We went with the tanks in this attack, falling flat as a shell burst, the metal ziffing and the dirt clods lobbing over."

Hemingway describes a seige

"The war in Spain has produced few good pictures," LIFE lamented in 1937. "Many a cameraman has risked his life for action shots only to have them seized by the military." Early in the game, the editors learned to rely not only on courage but also on experts and good connections. They asked novelist Ernest Hemingway, who was working as a war correspondent in Spain, to caption a series of pictures clipped from a remarkable film, *The Spanish Earth*, which had been sponsored by U.S. writers John Dos Passos and Archibald MacLeish.

Hemingway's words prefigured the terse, poetic lines of his Spanish classic, *For Whom the Bell Tolls*, and began a felicitous relationship between the Nobel laureate and LIFE that lasted until his death in 1961. It was from this combatant's-eye view that millions of Americans got their first impression of what war was about.

"They came grinding and clanking, suddenly to rise like ships on a wave, hanging a moment in mechanical balance on the ridge."

"They go forward in the ultimate loneliness of what is known as contact."

"The close ones have a zipping whisper and the really close ones crack."

"The loud-speaker opens the program with the Republican national anthem, greeted with shots from Rebels, followed by dance music."

"Then comes a speech. If this is listened to in silence by the Rebels there will probably be more desertions that night."

"The villagers of Fuenteduena on the main Madrid-Valencia highway irrigate their lands to grow food & wine for the soldiers."

"The family is dead. High in the sky and shining silver, death came to all who had no place to run, no place to hide."

"This is a man who had nothing to do with the war—a bookkeeper on his way to his office at eight o'clock in the morning."

"After the shelling boys hunt in the rubble for jagged metal or steel fragments and so the next shell ..."

"...finds them. The German artillery has increased their allowance per battery today."

Total war's first victims suffer in a lost cause

Robert Capa's famed photograph—"moment of death"—captures the instant a bullet crashes into the brain of a Republican militiaman.

Mouth open in rigor mortis, a Loyalist who was stringing telephone wires hangs in a tree after being shot by a Rebel sharpshooter.

Spanish refugees, including two children who each lost a leg in the fighting, move slowly down a road leading to sanctuary in France.

A stoic father, his cigar dead and forgotten in his mouth, carries his wounded son. The boy, reported LIFE, "has averted his tear-streaked face from the photographer."

Japanese conqueror

'Incident' in China

The "China Incident," as the Japanese called their assault on the Asian republic, was actually a full-scale conquest of Chinese territory comprising more square miles than the combined areas of Italy, Spain, France and Germany. It set the stage for World War II in the Far East, beginning in earnest with the capture of Peking and Tientsin in July 1937. As the fighting spread south to Shanghai and west to Hankow, the Japanese Army—originally 600,000 strong—lost 60,000 men, and slaughtered some two million Chinese.

The "incident" coincided with some of the early issues of LIFE. Unabashedly pro-Chinese, the editors nevertheless covered the Sino-Japanese War from both sides, assigning Japanese combat photographers as well as employing Americans like Robert Capa, whom they brought from the battlefields of Spain to China. In early 1938, the magazine stated its case for publishing pictures like those shown here: "The love of peace has no meaning unless it is based on a knowledge of war's terrors. Dead men have indeed died in vain if live men refuse to look at them."

◄ Wounded by a bomb, a Chinese baby howls pitifully in Shanghai's South Station. The famed picture, said LIFE, was seen by as many as 136,000,000 people.

Japanese soldiers wearing gas masks charge snipers holding out in Shanghai, which succumbed to the invaders ▼ only after a three-month struggle.

◄ The head of a Chinese soldier, frightening evidence of Japanese atrocities in Nanking, rests on a barbed-wire barricade that was erected in a futile effort to keep the invaders from reaching the city.

A Chinese child, casualty of the Japanese war, is carried to a stack of coffins hurriedly assembled to bury some of the thousands who lost their lives between 1937 and 1938.

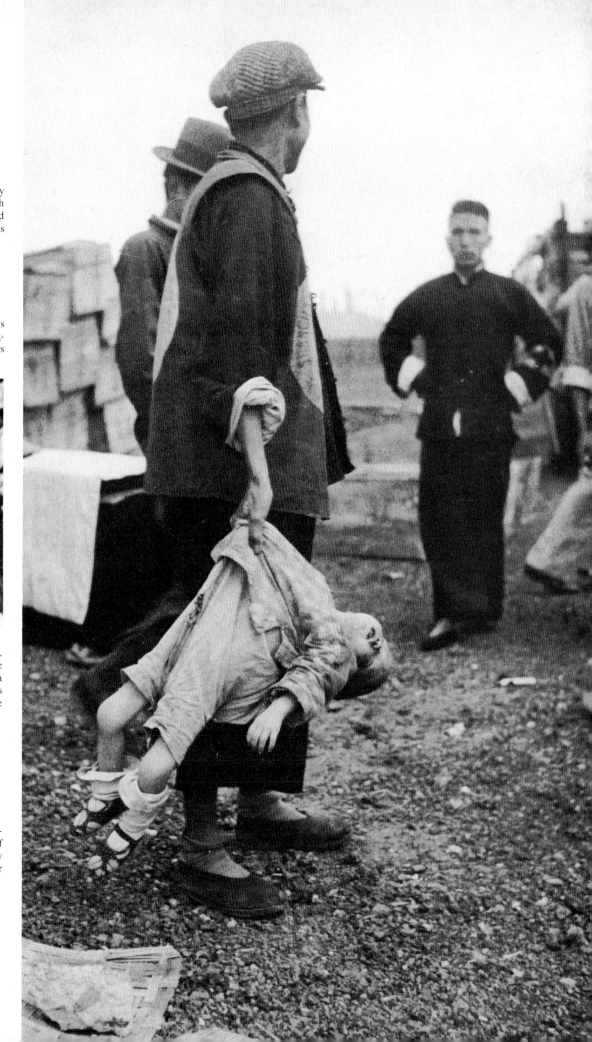

A jubilant Japanese general raises a cup of rice wine in a victory toast after the fall of Hsuchow, an industrial city in central China.

With a rousing "banzai," Japanese soldiers celebrate the occupation of Hankow's railway station. The photograph was taken for LIFE by American photographer Paul Dorsey, who got along so well with the Japanese that there was even a false rumor that he was in their pay. Dorsey had taken prewar pictures of Japan that were used in wartime issues of LIFE, when pictures of the enemy's home front were scarce.

Two old adversaries unite to fight a common enemy

The Japanese surge through China produced a historical odd couple: Chiang Kai-shek, leader of China's Nationalist government, and Communist chief Mao Tse-tung, bitter enemies who agreed to join forces in 1937 to battle the invader—a reconciliation that canceled the bounty that Chiang had offered for Mao's capture. LIFE covered both sides of this shotgun alliance, and shortly before it was forged, the magazine scored a journalistic coup by publishing the first photographs of Mao and his army *(opposite)*.

An American journalist named Edgar Snow was the source of the photographs. Snow had already spent eight years in China when he joined Mao and his Eighth Route Army men in the caves of Yenan, where they had fled to escape Nationalist forces in their historic Long March north. Snow became a friend and confidant of the revolutionary, photographed him in his now-famous unadorned uniform, and took candid shots of a bearded, obscure young Chou En-lai.

With as much optimism as it could muster, LIFE followed Chiang's military fortunes as his forces were overwhelmed, city by city, and as he retreated up the Yangtze gorges to his final wartime redoubt in Chungking. Noting his greatest humiliation after the fall of Hankow in 1938, the magazine reflected that Chiang, a converted Methodist, now had "for solace the examples of tribulation in the Christian Bible."

In 1926 Chiang takes tea with Mei-ling Soong, sister-in-law of the Chinese Republic's founder, Sun Yat-sen. They married in 1927.

Chiang *(center)* and his wife walk with Nationalist Army officers in 1928, the year he defeated rivals and consolidated his power.

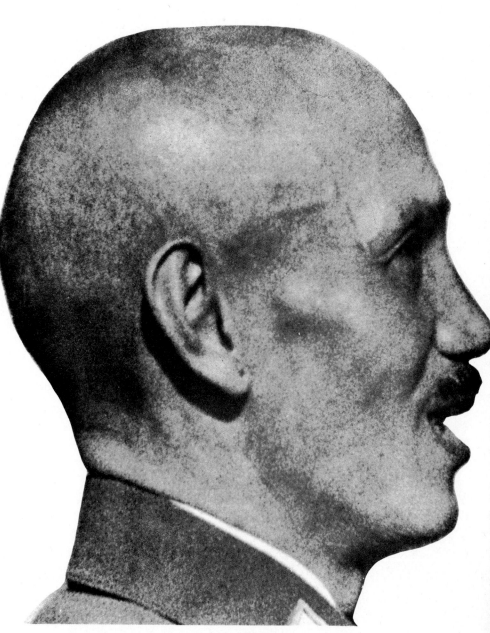

Dressed in civilian garb, Chiang and his staff stroll through a bamboo grove in western China, where he had fled to escape the Japanese.

This picture, captioned "hero of the ▲ week," appeared in LIFE's sixth issue in 1936, lauding Chiang for bringing order to a feudal nation.

A contingent of Communist cadets in ▲ sandals forms up at the Red Military Academy, which Mao ordered built in the wilds of Kiangsi Province.

In the dim light of an earthen hut, Red Army cadets bend over books—a chore often interrupted by forays against nearby Japanese troops.

◄ "Mao is his name and $250,000 the price on his head," LIFE captioned this picture of Mao, taken just before his uneasy truce with Chiang.

Communist troops enter a field hospital carved into the side of a hill in Shensi, the remote province Mao used as a base of operations.

Il Duce emergent

Germany resurgent

Rome-Berlin Axis

In 1938, two men, each the godhead of his own totalitarian faith, stood on a grassy Italian slope overlooking the Mediterranean and plotted the conquest of Europe. It was not their first meeting *(shown below)*, nor was it the last in a series that would go on for almost a decade.

Hitler had admired Il Duce from the first days of his own career—even before Mussolini had taken power in Italy. The source of the admiration was the Italian dictator's violent style, and in the early bully-boy phases of the Nazi Party, Hitler had himself introduced at political rallies as "Germany's Mussolini."

But Il Duce was never able to work up much fellow feeling for the Führer, despite the fact that both had come from poor families and had risen to power against the entrenched traditional ruling circles in their countries. When Hitler asked Mussolini for an autographed picture in the late 1920s, he was rudely turned down. After meeting Hitler in 1934, Mussolini called him a "mad little clown," and as late as 1938 referred to him in private as "that damned German." But Hitler's greater political effectiveness and his growing military power made Il Duce dependent on him. By the outbreak of World War II, the Italian leader had become a fawning puppet who had adopted a good many elements of the traditional German military ritual, including the goose step.

An admirer meets his idol

Alfred Eisenstaedt's historic photograph of the introduction of Hitler to Mussolini underlined the fact that the encounter was hardly between equals. Seeking an ally, Hitler had petitioned Il Duce for a conference, and had been invited to Venice, though Mussolini's motive in doing so was primarily curiosity to see the most talked-about political figure in Europe.

The get-together was not a success. In his worn trenchcoat, Hitler looked shabby beside Mussolini. Il Duce spoke loudly in accented German that Hitler found impossible to understand. At a Fascist gathering at the Piazza San Marco, Mussolini displayed himself on a prominent balcony, exiling Hitler to an inferior one. At their final meeting during the conference, Hitler talked too long and Il Duce walked out on him. Mussolini, said an aide, "was so bored by Hitler's drivel that . . . in the middle of the official reception, he decamped in a hurry . . . stating that he did not want to see anybody."

Hitler makes a seaside speech to Mussolini (holding a rose) and aides. Taken by one of the Führer's personal photographers, the picture did not appear in LIFE until 1970 because the cameraman had buried his pictures to hide them from American occupation troops in 1945.

A modern Caesar emerges

In 1938 LIFE's readers got a lengthy look at Mussolini in a detailed pictorial history that followed him from childhood to his ascension as Italy's dictator. They learned that Mussolini was born to a blacksmith-anarchist father and a socialist-teacher mother, from whose classroom "Benito may have drawn a first inspiration for totalitarian rule." Young Mussolini was pictured as a draft dodger, a starving vagrant who boasted that he was capable of murder, and an ardent socialist who denounced Italy's ruling class and edited the Left-Wing weekly *The Class Struggle.*

At 29, Mussolini spent time in jail for causing workers' riots, was drafted into the army during World War I and was wounded (in the rump, LIFE said). He returned home and started a new political movement that he called Fascism. By 1922, following his celebrated march on Rome, he had seized power from the weak parliamentary monarchy. A superb manipulator of large crowds, Mussolini was the very definition, LIFE put it, of the "Fascist Superman."

Mussolini flashes the piercing eyes of a firebrand Left-Winger in this formal portrait made in 1904.

In 1905, Private Mussolini sports a mustache and wears the feathered hat of an Italian elite regiment.

A scruffy infantryman in 1915, Mussolini *(center)* shares a bottle of wine with comrades in the Alps. Although eventually promoted to the rank of sergeant, Mussolini was a static soldier who rarely saw action.

Mussolini, now Premier, tussles with a lion cub in a staged photograph designed to boost his superman image.

Striking a characteristic pose in a baggy swim suit, a vacationing Mussolini dominates a beach.

Backing League of Nations status for Ethiopia in 1924, Mussolini poses in Geneva with Haile Selassie, the diminutive Ethiopian emperor, whose primitive nation Il Duce would later ruthlessly attack.

A bemedaled Mussolini and a coterie of Fascist cronies join Papal officials in Rome's Vatican City in 1929 after the astute Duce buried his dislike of Catholicism by signing a peace pact with Pope Piux XI.

Troublemaker Mussolini suffers arrest—one of the numerous times his politics landed him in jail.

At the pinnacle of power in 1938, a ▶ uniformed Il Duce performs what LIFE called his "Mussolini act."

LIFE captioned this 1928 photograph, also taken on a beach: "The great thinker, alone with the sea."

Outfitted in an Army uniform, Mussolini welcomes Emmy Göring, wife of Hitler's Luftwaffe chief. ▼ ▶

Hitler climbs on high

If it was hard not to think of Mussolini as a buffoon, it was harder still not to be deadly serious about Adolf Hitler. LIFE branded him a despot who was "allergic to the universe," a madman who "listened to voices, particularly his own, believed every word he heard and understood none." Yet the magazine diligently traced Hitler's "crooked" family tree in at least three picture biographies. (Sample item: His father was a bastard who probably married his niece.) In its first year of publication, LIFE ran photographs that showed Hitler as a wide-eyed toddler, an innocent-looking schoolboy in Austria, and a stern World War I corporal who refused to believe that Germany had lost the war. Other early issues carried photographs of Hitler in the 1920s with the roughneck Brownshirts who helped him in his rise.

A perfectionist where his person was concerned, Hitler insisted on milking his public appearances—like the one at left—for their maximum propaganda value. He made sure that only flattering pictures were published, and favored those in which he looked suitably heroic, giving the Nazi salute to throngs, playing the concerned father figure to countless children or being mobbed by adoring women.

In Munich at the outbreak of World War I, a mustachioed Corporal Hitler relaxes with comrades in the 16th Bavarian Reserve Infantry.

Flanked by storm troopers, Adolf Hitler makes a triumphant entry at a rally held at Bückeburg. The culmination of such spectaculars, often involving hundreds of thousands, came when the Führer mounted his platform, as LIFE put it, to "harangue into hysterics his acres of followers."

A ruthless crowd-pleaser arises to challenge the world

With the Nazi rabble-rouser Julius Streicher at his side, Hitler leads a tumultuous march through Munich.

In 1923, Hitler poses with Army officers who joined him in a futile attempt to seize power.

Hitler passes through an honor guard of motley-uniformed Nazis after delivering a speech to party members.

At a 1927 Nuremburg rally, Hitler "heils" to the faithful from the front of an open Mercedes-Benz.

Hitler looks across the North Sea to England, some 300 miles away, in this Nazi propaganda photo.

After being named Chancellor in 1933, Hitler bows to Weimar Republic President Hindenburg.

A jovial Führer banters with German industrialists, whose factories he depended on to produce war matériel.

Hitler grins at a tiny Brownshirt whose dress, said LIFE, was a "childish mockery" of Nazism.

Admiring girls surround Hitler, who saw himself as a bachelor irresistibly attractive to women.

Men and machines warm up

Early in 1937, LIFE gave its readers a look at a newly bellicose Germany. That nation, led by Hitler and his two principal deputies—the portly, swaggering Hermann Göring and the crippled, fanatical Joseph Goebbels—was already well along the road to war. Germany had torn up the Treaty of Versailles, had begun to build modern war machines, though equipment was still primitive, and had introduced conscription. In defiance of Treaty clauses that had demilitarized the Rhineland, Nazi troops had marched into the West German region and occupied it.

This development must have particularly gratified Goebbels, a Rhinelander who had joined the Nazi Party in 1924. By 1937, his genius for propaganda had enabled him to draw the press and every other source of information available to Germans into his own hands, along with control of most of the nation's artistic and cultural institutions. Goebbels did not regulate the armed forces, which Göring considered his own sphere of influence. A wealthy World War I ace who had helped the infant Nazi Party with money and contacts among the aristocracy, Göring by 1937 was in the process of building the world's mightiest air force and was also in charge of organizing finances for German rearmament.

Fists clenched, hefty Hermann Göring, a veteran of the famous von Richthofen Squadron of World War I, bellows into a microphone.

30

In this photograph by Margaret Bourke-White, ersatz tanks, jalopies with tin sides and wood guns, lumber across a field on maneuvers.

Paul Joseph Goebbels reads to his daughters, whom at war's end he put to death just before he and his wife committed suicide. ▼

A British photographer took this picture of the club-footed Goebbels, who later banned any mention of his deformity in the German press. ▶

1936-1939

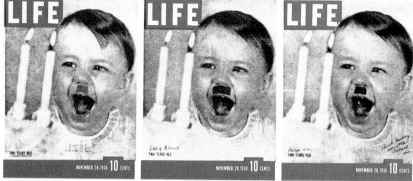

Readers adorned LIFE's second anniversary baby cover with Hitlerian mustaches.

Hijinks Over Here

Americans greeted the Hitler myth with indulgent ridicule—or just ignored it. People were more excited about the new World's Fair under construction in New York's Flushing Meadow, about swing and the Big Band sound, and about a new dance craze, the Big Apple, and its stutter-step number called Truckin' than they were about political happenings unfolding in Europe.

To most in the U.S. these events seemed comfortably remote, and times at home were still hard; Americans were looking for something to distract, titillate or entertain them. When LIFE celebrated its second anniversary with a picture of a two-year-old girl from Pennsylvania, many readers noted that she parted her hair on the wrong side like Hitler. They painted a toothbrush mustache on her and sent her picture back to LIFE by the dozens. LIFE also covered students goose-stepping at a University of West Virginia "Hitler ball" fraternity party that was a zany mockery of Third Reich rituals. At this gathering, the Grand Goose Step replaced the Grand March, "storm troopers" guzzled rootbeer and pretzels, and Brownshirt getups fashioned from Boy Scout and National Guard uniforms made "every man a Führer."

Make-believe Führers, one wearing a prewar spiked helmet, another a Boy Scout uniform, clown at a University of West Virginia frat party.

The Petty Girl, like this 1938 version of the popular pin-up art, exuded homespun sexuality on the walls of fraternity houses all over the country.

◄ An unfinished Trylon and Perisphere are reflected in a pool at the New York World's Fair, which opened a few months before war broke out.

West Point in 1938 was preoccupied by cadet marriages like this one, and LIFE noted that 30 grads made wives of 30 pretty spinsters that June.

Two women clad in Big-Apple-print dresses demonstrate the step as part of a nationwide Applemania that even turned up in housecoat patterns.

At Camp Siegfried on Long Island, an incipient Nazi eyes the camera while his elders give the Nazi salute. The Bund claimed 200,000 members in the U.S.

Homegrown Hitlers sprout as a brief nuisance

A spin-off of Hitler's Germany that did not amuse most Americans was the transplanted Nazi Party. The American Nazis were the creation of a group called the German-American Bund. Run by a one-time Ford Motor Company chemist named Fritz Kuhn, the party drew most of its members from the German immigrant Yorkville section of New York City.

Up to a point, the Bund—and other homegrown racist and fascist organizations—were protected by the U.S. Constitution, and its "storm troopers" were free to "heil" mini-führers in suburban beer gardens and local meeting halls. Some found this activity merely ludicrous; one anti-Nazi quipped that Hitler youth camps were springing up "where little uniformed Nazi cherubs learn to goose-step and see how far they can horn into the Boy Scouts." But LIFE was less easygoing about the Nazi presence. It warned that in addition to agitating against American Jews, the movement was a "hydra-headed menace," a fifth column that could threaten the security of the United States itself.

A Bundist functionary salutes his audience at a 1938 rally. Characteristically, he is flanked by American and Nazi flags and George Washington, who was hailed as "the first fascist."

Press photographers were barred ▶ from places like Camp Siegfried, but a LIFE representative sneaked out this shot of members of the German-American Bund up a tree. They were part of the uniformed *Ordnungs Dienst* (Order Guard). "American citizens," commented LIFE, "were getting fed up with such fifth column monkeyshines, whether in treetops or on drill grounds."

NO DO IN WATER

Wooden guns, aerial mishaps and skeleton crews define the

▲ A squad trains with a wood tripod as a 60mm mortar. This picture was used in LIFE with an official Army report on military preparedness.

A makeshift field gun—a plank laid across old wagon wheels—was the best the underweaponed Army could ▼ come up with for combat maneuvers.

"This Is Half of the U.S. Army's Only Mechanized Cavalry Brigade," ran LIFE's headline over these two pictures in 1938. Actually one photo-

Nose ignominiously buried in the ground, a prototype Boeing YB-17 Flying Fortress rests in a field after ▼ crashing during a test flight. "Too

much plane for any ordinary pilot to handle," was the comment of some airmen. The first Fortress crashed in 1935, killing two of its crew.

state of America's preparedness: poverty-stricken

graph torn in two, it is shown here just as it was in the magazine. The armed services were delighted with such layouts in LIFE, whose editors, exposed to continual reports from its overseas correspondents of Axis military resurgence, were genuinely alarmed at America's unreadiness. LIFE hoped its saber rattling would prod its readers and Congress into acknowledging a rapidly expanding German fighting force.

French commander Gamelin

Pomp As Usual

On the Continent, mere borders separated nations from attack by Hitler. Britain, protected by the English Channel and buttressed by its empire, could feel only slightly more secure. But hardly anybody in either place was willing to believe that Herr Hitler might be a threat to the West. This heedless mood came through in pictures of military pomp and ceremony that showed the West turning its back on the German menace.

LIFE made fun of the world's only military bicycle band in Holland and of Britain's elite dragoons, one of whose members was shown kissing his nag goodbye—since his unit was, as a sign of the times, converting to vehicles. Even the British Navy came in for some gentle ridicule. As British warships strung with lightbulbs for the coronation of King George VI were suddenly illuminated, an enthusiastic BBC announcer shouted, "Damme, the fleet is all lit up!" Soon all England was chanting the line, with its merrymaking overtones.

Across the Channel in France, the mood was only scarcely more realistic. The French went about their business, placing total confidence in their magnificent Maginot Line, which LIFE inspected in a detailed photo-essay and pronounced capable of stopping any invader in his tracks.

All spit and polish, a Royal Enniskillen Dragoon Guard kisses his horse goodbye after his regiment was mechanized by the War Office.

This tuba-tootling member of Holland's bicycle band, chortled LIFE, "definitely dislikes rough roads, positively dreads blowouts."

On May 20, 1937, a Royal Navy warship blazes with lights during fleet celebrations for Britain's newly crowned King George VI.

Reflecting the proper imperial image, a British major and his lady in Rajputana, India, ride to their wedding on a decorated elephant.

Maginot Line pillboxes were part of a $400 million complex that LIFE said "will prevent any such sweeping advance as was seen in 1914."

1936-1939

Artful appeaser

A Futile Dream: 'Peace for Our Time'

"If Hitler does not double-cross Britain now, Germany's future looks brighter than ever before in modern history." With these words in October 1938, LIFE echoed the relief felt in Europe and America on the return from Munich of British Prime Minister Neville Chamberlain. In a kind of shuttle diplomacy, the austere Briton had flown back and forth to Germany three times to see Hitler. On September 30, he landed in England to announce a pact with the Führer that would, he said, guarantee "peace for our time." Whatever his critics (Churchill on the one hand and British leftists on the other) said about his "betrayal" of the Czechs, whose country he had agreed to let Hitler split up, Chamberlain had bought time for Britain to rearm. Of far more importance, LIFE thought wishfully, Chamberlain "for the first time succeeded in winning Germany back to the democratic principle of collective bargaining, involving it once more in the web of legal civilized procedure." When peace collapsed a year later and Chamberlain was exhausted and ill, LIFE implied that he was in such disrepute that he had to slip into his official residence at 10 Downing Street by a rear entrance.

Chamberlain confers with his Foreign Secretary, Lord Halifax *(above)*, before flying to see Hitler. At right, he returns in triumph to London's Heston Aerodrome after signing the pact with Hitler that he believed would stave off war—despite warnings from British intelligence that Hitler was preparing for a major thrust throughout Russia and Western Europe.

An enterprising photographer caught Chamberlain and his wife entering No. 10 Downing Street by a back door one year after Munich.

In greasepaint mustache and makeshift wing collar, a British actor spoofs Neville Chamberlain. The impersonation was part of a savagely satirical skit called *Babes in the Wood*, which reflected a significant and skeptical body of British opinion.

A London newsboy hawks papers that announce Chamberlain's peace, which LIFE called "the biggest news in the world."

Bloodless Conquests

Czech chief Syrovy

Hitler consciously pushed his country ever closer to war as the Thirties drew to a close. His bluff and threat had already led him to march into the "demilitarized" Rhineland in 1936 and had given him Austria in a bloodless *Anschluss*. Emboldened by these successes and anxious to test the still-untried German army, Hitler turned bellicose eyes toward Czechoslovakia, which an aide said he was determined to crush militarily "even at the risk of a world war."

But to Hitler's chagrin, the Wehrmacht was denied its moment of glory by Chamberlain's offer of Czechoslovakia's heavily fortified Sudetenland. The victim was thus stripped of its defensive buffer and its army demoralized. Its pathetic civilian defense was epitomized by children playing in gas masks *(right)*. Prague, the Czech capital, fell on March 15, 1939, without a shot being fired.

LIFE covered the bewildering rush of events and grudgingly admitted that Hitler had "if not military genius, considerable political talent." Genius or not, Hitler would shortly switch from political coercion to the military force he had been prepared to turn loose all along.

Standing in a six-wheeled army car, Hitler basks in the adulation of his fellow Austrians in Vienna, two days after the capital fell.

In Czechoslovakia's Sudetenland, Hitler rides in triumph down a flower-strewn street lined with saluting and cheering people. ▼

In 1938 LIFE showed these Czech ▶ boys in a camp near Prague, "learning to play games in the stuffy semisecurity of rubberized gas masks."

Enter Joseph Stalin

Like much of the rest of the world, LIFE was fascinated and not a little perplexed by the former seminarian from the Republic of Georgia named Joseph Dzhugashvili. In an early issue, the magazine traced his life in romanticized paintings supplied by a Soviet picture agency, noting that young Joseph "was a born scrapper, got himself a black eye once a month." The scrapper rose rapidly with the Bolsheviks and, after Lenin died in 1924, made himself absolute dictator of Russia.

Now known by his revolutionary name Stalin (steel), he proved to be a volatile leader who could play the gregarious Russian bear while brutally purging his enemies. Among them was Red Army leader Leon Trotsky, who fled Russia and ended up in exile in Mexico, where he wrote a scathing account for LIFE of Stalin's rise to power.

After failing to achieve any assurances of collective action against Germany from Britain or France, Stalin startled—and angered—them by signing the nonaggression pact with Hitler in August 1939. That set the stage for the outbreak of war a month later. "The high priests of the two great new rival political religions of the 20th Century," said LIFE, "reveal themselves as nothing after all but a pair of hardboiled and practical nationalist bosses."

An early photograph of Stalin shows the Georgian with an ailing Lenin, who when healthy actively shunned his power-hungry lieutenant.

Caught by the camera in a benevolent mood in 1938, Stalin shares a private joke with two babushkaed and giggling collective farmers.

All business, Stalin dictates a note to his chief of staff during the conferences that led up to the nonaggression pact with Germany.

Trotsky on Stalin: 'He envied Hitler and secretly deferred to him'

Shortly after the signing of the Nazi-Soviet pact, LIFE *asked Leon Trotsky, "No. 1 Revolutionist" and exiled foe of Stalin, to assess the Red dictator. Trotsky wired the following brilliantly precise comments from Mexico City:*

Superficial psychologists represent Stalin as a perfectly poised being, as something like a child of nature. In reality, he consists entirely of contradictions. The most significant of these is the discrepancy between his ambitious will and his resources of intellect and talent. What characterized Lenin was the harmony of his psychic forces: theoreti-

cal mind, practical sagacity, strong will, endurance. All this was tied up in one active whole.... The strength of Stalin's will is not inferior perhaps to that of Lenin's but his intellectual capacities, as compared to Lenin's, measure only 10 or 20 per cent.... The hate for the powerful of this world was always his main driving force as a revolutionary, rather than the sympathy for the oppressed.... At the same time, he is hypersensitive, easily offended and capricious. Feeling himself pushed aside, he turns his back, hides in a corner and smokes his pipe, is morosely silent and dreams of revenge....

Stalin is the most outstanding mediocrity of the Soviet bureaucracy. His strength lies in the fact that he expresses the instinct of self-preservation of the ruling caste more firmly, more decisively, and more pitilessly than anyone else. But that is also his weakness. He sees clearly for a short distance, but on a historical scale he is blind. A shrewd tactician, he is not a strategist.... Stalin carried in himself the consciousness of his mediocrity. Hence, his need for flattery. Hence, his envy of Hitler and the secret deference ... inspired in him by the German genius with the mustache of Charlie Chaplin.

45

Displays of might and patriotism presage European bloodshed

A German 88mm antiaircraft gun belches smoke and fire during 1938 tests at Nuremburg in which Hitler brandished his new weaponry.

Displaying a very stiff upper lip, a Welsh matron epitomizes the ordinary Briton's patriotic aversion to potential foes like Hitler. For all her determination, LIFE noted, she had ▶ inadvertently pinned the Union Jack on upside down, "which on land or sea is a signal of distress."

1939

Nazi nabobs

A better bomber

R.A.F. stinger

Mechanized cavalryman

British WAAF officer

Fledgling paratrooper

First line of defense

Biggest gun

A British tar in the U.S.

1941

Distaff warrior

British sky shield

Airborne infantryman

Aussies in Africa

Noble naval hero

Desert Rats

II.   AXIS ONSLAUGHT

Hitler unleashes a new brand of mobile war

The generals and the admirals, says Clausewitz, are always prepared to fight the previous conflict. When the Stukas screamed down out of Poland's clear dawn sky on September 1, 1939, without a declaration of war, the military experts whipped out their manuals, but it was quickly apparent that the German high command had thrown away the book. Their swift stabs left no time for the trenches of World War I, as the Wehrmacht's armor raced along the highways while its air partner was smashing fortifications, supply bases and airfields.

Flaunting his dazzling one-month victory in Poland, Hitler tried to make a deal with England and France so that he could go after his real dream: the riches of Russia. But France took up a World War I defense posture in the Maginot Line and Britain sent the British Expeditionary Force under Lord Gort to dig in where the Maginot concrete fell short of the sea. Their hopes for a stalemate were shattered. In April 1940, after the six-month breather dubbed Sitzkrieg, Hitler turned on Denmark, Norway, Holland and Belgium and rolled through Flanders, sweeping the BEF and French defenders to the edge of the sea at Dunkirk.

The epic evacuation of those men off Dunkirk's beaches galvanized Britain into the force that Hitler had feared it would become. Inspired by the heroic cadences of their new warrior Prime Minister, Winston Churchill ("I have nothing to offer but blood, toil, tears and sweat"), Britons shucked their illusions of "peace for our time" and went about the business of defending their homes. For the Germans, the precondition for the invasion of England was the destruction of the R.A.F. In Operation Eagle, Hermann Göring set about the job systematically. He came within an ace of success, but then suddenly relieved the exhausted Fighter Command by switching his raiders to civilian targets—notably London. He lost the battle, and Hitler called off the invasion.

The Soviets, after an embarrassingly difficult winter struggle to defeat Finland, had tightened their Baltic defenses. Hitler was deterred once again from attacking the Soviets, this time by the need to bail out his hapless ally Mussolini in Greece and North Africa. But the invasion of Russia finally got underway and Joseph Stalin

(Sta-a-rlin, as Churchill called him on the BBC) was overnight the Prime Minister's "gallant ally." Reinforced by his third-term vote of confidence, Franklin Roosevelt promptly pushed through his Lend-Lease Bill and "the great arsenal of democracy" slowly began to deliver up its weaponry to the Allies. The Red Army learned that power lay in its superior numbers of fighting men and not in land, and fell back across "scorched earth" to fight deep inside Mother Russia.

Through blitzkrieg and Sitzkrieg, Winter War and desert war, LIFE exuberantly pursued two newfound missions: serving as the nation's guide to military development and probing the moods of a people not yet awake to the implications of a world conflict. It elucidated the workings of every weapon, every vehicle and every branch of the service. It produced a *Dictionary of Modern Warfare.* It demonstrated "How to Fight Dirty" and, in Gjon Mili stroboscope sequences, how to fall down and fire the new M-1 rifle. It published detailed maps of campaigns and battles, always under deadline pressure and often under the handicap of military censorship that made the maps incomplete or flawed.

LIFE showed how it was to be a Londoner under the blitz, a Parisian when Nazi boots pounded down the Champs Elysées. In London, the staff rotated as air-raid wardens, sometimes slept in the office basement, sometimes went home and got bombed out. The Paris bureau fled to Bordeaux and came close, along the way, to being lynched by humiliated Frenchmen for trying to photograph the exodus.

On the domestic front, the magazine reported America's stubborn neutrality, but worked hard to involve Americans first in aid to Britain, then in war production for the Allies. It staged an "imaginary invasion" of England. It told how Lexington, Massachusetts, and Hamilton, Ohio (a favorite "mid-America" town whose pulse the editors loved to take), were girding to fight Nazi spies and saboteurs.

The magazine played these themes against the counterpoint of a nation still very much at peace: jazz musician Gene Krupa drumming, baseball star Ted Williams hitting home runs, college football great Tommy Harmon scoring touchdowns and New York's Mayor Fiorello LaGuardia chasing fire engines. These notes blended with the piccolo tootlings of campus foolishness, the trumpet blasts of a new labor militancy and the patter of the Hollywood barker touting the beautiful women and godlike men of the movie capital. Beneath all the cacophony, however, was a deeper note, sounded with increasing volume, that would summon the ordinary people of America to fight on distant shores against an enemy increasingly seen as menacing and evil.

Poland's invader

Blitzkrieg in Poland

Hitler selected Poland, his Slavic neighbor to the east, to demonstrate to Europe the terrible punishment packed by the new kind of warfare his air and ground forces had worked to perfect in Spain. Within the first few days of his sudden strike across the German-Polish border on September 1, 1939, the world became familiar with two words that had until then been German military jargon: *blitzkrieg,* or lightning war, and *Panzer,* the tank and motorized infantry forces that combined with bombers to wage it.

On September 1 the Panzer divisions swept across the Polish frontier in a pincer movement, converging on Warsaw. On the 5th the first bombers appeared over the capital and wiped out air bases and bridges. But the Luftwaffe's mission was to destroy the city utterly, and a week later it was systematically pursuing that mission, sending over wave after wave of high-level planes and screaming Stuka dive bombers.

A special war issue, in which LIFE printed the first wire-photo pictures of war-shattered Poland, reported that incendiary bombs had set great fires raging, that women were digging trenches and laying land mines, that more civilians than soldiers had died and that the streets were littered with corpses. Four weeks after the launching of one of history's fastest military campaigns, Warsaw had fallen and the last resistance in Poland had been extinguished.

Polish civilians gaze fearfully at a sky that is full of German bombers; as many as 60 or 70 in a wave rained death on Warsaw.

On the ground, Nazis penetrate Warsaw's outskirts with *(from left)* a machine gun, a howitzer, a motorcycle and a medium tank.

Germans "purifying" conquered Poland round up young Jews in Warsaw. Some captives were sent to ghettos, but the purge had begun.

Imposing discipline by terror, German MPs march Poles through a Silesian town (whose German minority owns the shops at right) and *(below)* shoot three prisoners. Poland claimed that 25,000 were executed in four months.

During the Polish campaign, Hitler and his Foreign Minister, Joachim von Ribbentrop, stroll along a muddy road on a visit to conquered territory. LIFE, featuring the photograph as Picture of the Week, noted that the Führer took the high ground while Ribbentrop walked in the mud.

U.S. Reaction: Nuttiness and Neutrality

The news that Europe was erupting into war caught the U.S. in its usual end-of-summer zaniness. Reviewing the period in a story headlined "The Week the War Began," LIFE quoted industrialist Henry Ford, who said there would be no war in Europe. Also reported in the article: Women were up in arms over the return of the corset; and 65-year-old Interior Secretary Harold Ickes' 26-year-old bride bore a son.

Shortly thereafter, President Roosevelt, endangering his campaign for an unprecedented third term, asked for repeal of the Neutrality Act (which barred arms shipments to any belligerent) and triggered a massive outpouring of Keep-America-Out-of-It mail. Even as it inundated Congress, which noted an anti-repeal majority variously estimated at from 2-to-1 to 20-to-1, normal September life went on. Indeed, its trivial aspects, LIFE philosophized, "acquired suddenly a strange importance. Against the background of war, they emerged sharp and impressive ... like a familiar landscape made clear by lightning in the summer night."

At their Chicago convention, American Legionnaires, refusing to let the war inhibit their tomfoolery, hoist chorus girls. They voted to stay out of the war, but, on the Neutrality Act, remained uncommitted.

Hollywood's four Lane Sisters carry placards to protest the new French wasp-waist corset, which, along with the bustle, had been resurrected in Paris, a city where the arbiters of fashion were still in business.

"Two Ton" Tony Galento, boxing's No. 2 (to Joe Louis), training for a fight, makes an unlikely Tarzan.

Fanny Brice and Gracie Allen race on trikes at a party given by Miss Allen for radio's Baby Snooks.

Pro-neutrality letters pile up in the Senate mail room. They came in at the rate of more than 200,000 a day.

Dancer Bill "Bojangles" Robinson immortalizes his footprints in cement at the New York World's Fair.

Eleanor Holm, star of the Fair's Aquacade, the spectacle run by husband Billy Rose, dazzles the Navy.

A giant postcard bears the sentiments of 700 Iowans who signed it and sent it to their Senator, Guy M. Gillette.

New York's Senator Robert F. Wagner received more than 20,000 pieces of antiwar mail in one morning.

Americans on the steps of the Capitol listen to the radio broadcast of F.D.R.'s September 21 plea that the

arms embargo be repealed so that the U.S. could come to the aid of countries fighting the Axis.

Ginger Rogers gingerly cuddles a pigeon in *Fifth Avenue Girl*, her comedy that was packing the movie

houses. The other smash hit of the season was Judy Garland's classic musical *The Wizard of Oz*.

Sarah Palfrey makes a balletic leap in her losing Wightman Cup Match against England's Valerie Scott.

In Oakland, California, airline stewardesses buck the neutrality trend, joining the Army Nurses Reserve. ▼

A license plate sports an antiwar tag distributed by Hearst's isolationist *New York Journal-American*.

At a Fort Wayne, Indiana, twins' convention, Florence and Alberta Spaeth were named "most unalike."

England: Facing Up

The very day the Wehrmacht rolled, Britain acted. The first thought of the imperiled nation was for its children. Youngsters aged four to 16 were picked up from bomb-target cities—in carts, in prams, on foot, by bus and by train, some with parents, most with teachers and nurses. They were then packed off to camps and houses in rural areas. In the first three days of September, 650,000 children were evacuated from London alone. The mothers of schoolchildren, forbidden to see them off and not knowing where they were being taken, crowded weeping outside railroad stations.

"I will not wage a fight against women and children," Hitler said in his war message to the Reichstag. But as he spoke, LIFE reported, German planes were dropping bombs on women and children in Polish cities. The magazine pointed out that this was not sheer hypocrisy: in modern war every industrial city was a military objective. The magazine showed the practice blackouts and air-raid drills that London was running, and the "knitting offensive" that the home front, remembering the trenches of World War I, was mounting to keep its warriors warm and dry.

Londoners in a practice air-raid drill go "back to the cave," as LIFE, unable to resist dramatizing, put it. At left are concrete bomb shelters.

NIGHT

The lights go out in London. The scenes are two stages of a practice blackout at the same intersection. Billboards, legible in the normal

London children, tagged with I.D.s and clutching their belongings, including compulsory—and frightening—gas masks, await evacuation.

A London cabbie and a concerned oldster ply patriotic knitting needles—a home-front theme that LIFE would vary throughout the war.

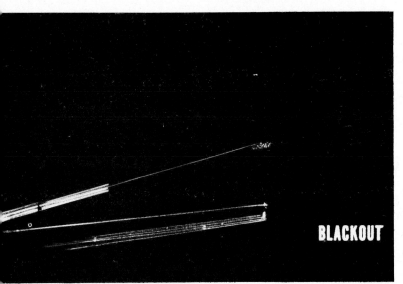

BLACKOUT

night view, are invisible in the blackout shown above. The only lights left are dimmed automobile headlights and traffic lanterns.

French defender

The Sit-down War

From the outbreak of war, Hitler—attacking to the east—had felt a gnawing anxiety about his vulnerable western rear. Thus the dazzling speed of Germany's destruction of Poland arose not only from Hitler's desire to overawe Europe with his Panzers, but also from his need—since Britain and France had declared war within two days of the Polish invasion—to transfer his troops as fast as possible to his western frontier. During his attack eastward, he had kept only minimal forces manning the Siegfried Line, a 30-mile-deep belt of underground concrete bunkers, steel antitank barriers and sunken gun emplacements. This system of fortifications faced its French mirror image, the Maginot Line, across the border from Switzerland to Belgium.

But Hitler needn't have hurried. The French, feeling secure behind the Maginot, had prepared for a defensive war. For eight months the war in the West was a sedentary "twilight" stalemate (which Americans promptly dubbed the Phony War and Europeans called the sitzkrieg). To the soldiers manning the lines, the principal dangers were ennui and lack of sunlight in underground bunkers.

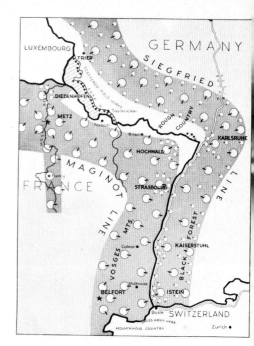

Blocking ancient invasion routes, Germany's Siegfried and France's Maginot lines blanket the Rhine and the mineral-rich Saar valley.

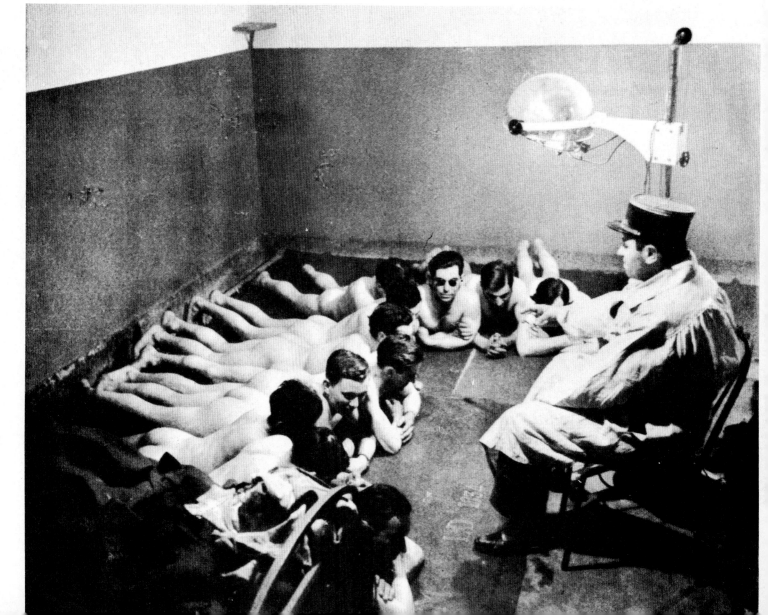

◄ French soldiers bathe in ultraviolet rays under the supervision of a doctor in a room 150 feet underground in the Maginot Line. Besides killing germs, the rays increased hemoglobin and combated what the Germans called *Bunkerkrankheit* (blockhouse fever)—boredom-induced blues.

A French GI, or poilu, sits out his stint near the Maginot Line. French faith in their defense system seems pathetic in hindsight. "The reason for the inaction," LIFE said, describing the poilu, "is precisely the terrible effectiveness of such weapons as his machine gun."

59

Interlude: the Crushing of Finland

The Soviet Union, seeking to expand into territory in which the terms of the Nazi-Soviet pact had given it a free hand, pressed Finland for territorial concessions on the Karelian Isthmus and elsewhere. When the former Russian grand duchy refused, the U.S.S.R. invaded on November 30, 1939, and the winter war began. The Red Army's mechanized forces hurled themselves against the fortifications of the Mannerheim Line and pushed their tanks and heavy equipment into forest roads farther north. The winter-wise Finns, usually on skis, moved easily through their familiar terrain. Although outmanned three to one, they nevertheless annihilated one Russian army and part of another, while American observers—not the least of them LIFE—cheered the doughty white-garbed defenders.

After a January pause, however, the Red Army renewed its assault. Moving its huge guns and tanks on fir-log roads built across frozen lakes, deploying its own ski infantry and subjecting Finnish cities to saturation bombing, it prevailed in short order. On March 12 Finland capitulated, having held out 105 days against 45 Soviet divisions.

A Finnish ski patrol, clad in white ▲ camouflage suits, unloads from a bus close to the front near Salla, where the Finns smashed a Russian force.

Outside a target village near Hango, a girl clutches her little sister while other children huddle close and gaze ▼ up at Soviet bombers.

A Russian bomber drops explosives on a Finnish town. Bombing forced daytime evacuation of towns and villages, impeding war production. The picture, like those below, is from a Soviet film documentary about the attack on the Finns' defensive Mannerheim Line, released one year later.

◄ A force of Red Army ski troops moves across the ice toward Koivisto Island, its tight formation indicating absence of Finnish airpower. Koivisto was the vital sea anchor of the Mannerheim Line.

A column of 30-ton tanks assembles behind the Russian line for an attack. Confined to roads by the snow, such columns were raided by skiborne Finns and, in northern Finland's forests, butchered. The Russians' mistake, LIFE said, was "to try a blitzkrieg in an impassable forest." But these pictures proved, the magazine added, that "the Red Army knows how to fight and how to die."

61

Blitzkrieg Encore: Attack in the West

German horse teams drawing 105mm howitzers rumble through a Norwegian town past a column of carts carrying ammunition.

Suddenly breaking the torpid winter spell of the sitzkrieg, the Germans struck Denmark, which capitulated in four hours, then Norway, Holland and Belgium in rapid succession. Reacting to the attack on Norway, the British got their first bitter lesson in coping with Nazi air superiority. In the first days, the Germans had captured all the best airfields, and when the British belatedly landed, the Nazis were able to blast their supply bases and airstrips and strafe the unprotected British columns. German troops landed from warships, in the first amphibious operation of the war, and met scant resistance from the Norwegians, who were undone by the sheer rapidity and faultless execution of the Nazi onslaught. Publishing its first pictures of the invasion, LIFE said: "The whole operation was run off by thoroughly trained executives who knew their men and machines." Industrial south Norway fell in 25 days and the whole country capitulated a month later.

Halfway through the Norwegian campaign, Germany launched one of history's most significant battles. At dawn on May 10, Hitler's paratroopers dropped on Holland. At about the same time, German gliders swooped down on the Belgian side of the Albert Canal, and within minutes key bridges were in German hands. Holland fell in four days. The Wehrmacht poured through Belgium to attack Sedan, at the northern tip of the Maginot line, and the Battle of Flanders, ending at Dunkirk on June 4, became the Battle of France.

A tank-supported German bicycle patrol, surprised by Norwegians firing from the hills, takes cover on the road behind the tank. Each bicycle carried two boxes of ammunition. Oslo was occupied the first day of the invasion, April 9, but the King had fled to the mountains.

Nazi assault troops, young, tough and disciplined, dart out from beneath railroad cars to attack Belgian defenders of the Albert Canal. In all, there were 240 German divisions, spearheaded by airborne shock troops. Fort Eban Emael, thought to be impregnable, was subdued in less than an hour by glider troops who dropped specially prepared explosives down the gun turrets, which spread flames and gas throughout.

Battle-tested defender

Churchill in Charge

When a serious-faced Winston Churchill appeared as First Lord of the Admiralty on LIFE's cover in 1940, the attack on England he had long warned about was only weeks away. Though he had a reputation as a Cassandra, Churchill brought dazzling credentials to his new office: Sandhurst graduate; cavalry officer; writer; successively a correspondent, prisoner and cavalry lieutenant in the Boer War (captured in his war-correspondent uniform, he escaped PW camp, then asked for and got his old commission back); Tory M.P.; Liberal Cabinet Minister; and World War I First Lord of the Admiralty. He had prepared the Grand Fleet for war, then took the blame in 1915 for the vain attempt to force the Dardanelles against the Turks at Gallipoli.

After beginning his second stint at the Admiralty, he soon added the post of chief of the Supreme Defense Council, and by mid-May of 1940 he was Prime Minister, in complete command of Britain's conduct of the war against Germany.

In 1894, Winston Leonard Spencer Churchill (left) was a fresh-faced 20-year-old cadet at the Royal Military Academy at Sandhurst.

As cabinet member at 35, in diplomatic uniform, Churchill attended German military maneuvers and shook hands with Kaiser Wilhelm.

Home Secretary Churchill rode with Clementine, his Scottish wife, in George V's coronation parade following Edward VII's death.

A dashing First Lord of the Admiralty in World War I, Churchill learned to pilot the Navy's rickety planes and flew all over England.

Watched by Clementine, Churchill in 1939 pursued one of his favorite avocations, painting on the lawn at Chartwell, his estate in Kent.

Lieutenant Churchill, on leave from the cavalry, served in Cuba in 1895, aiding Spain against the U.S. Later he rejoined his regiment in India.

Already a skillful political speaker, Churchill was elected to Parliament at the age of 25 as a Tory from the borough of Oldham.

Churchill in 1899 was a Lieutenant of the South African Light Horse. His brother Jack, later a World War I hero, was wounded at his side.

Cabinet Minister in 1908, Churchill ran in Manchester to keep his Parliamentary seat. He lost, but was invited to run in Dundee, where he won.

At Chartwell, in 1939, before the war broke out, Great Britain's leader-to-be built a brick wall, another one of his beloved pastimes.

Churchill reads the paper late in 1940, when good news was victory over Italians in Africa. Warning Britons not to celebrate, he said, "I do not recollect that we had any important occasion for rejoicing in the last war, but the people seemed pleased at the way it ended."

French loser Weygand

The German Sweep across France

Punching through the Ardennes near Sedan, the Germans outflanked the Maginot Line and poured over the Meuse River. French forces were pinned down by Stukas that dive-bombed their columns and plastered their rail and communication lines, while Luftwaffe fighters kept the R.A.F. and French Air Force from taking out the bridges.

On the ground, the Germans stopped French tanks with 1½-inch antitank guns, which the French lacked, although the Dutch and the Belgians had deployed excellent 2-inch guns. In desperation, the French turned to the unwieldy 3-inch 75s of World War I. But the key to victory was the individual soldiers, as illustrated below. Drilled to work together, German infantrymen followed the tanks and secured the countryside with remarkable speed.

The spearhead German force knifed across the top of France, in the rear of the northern Allied armies, then closed in to hem them in along the coast. The entrapped contingents appeared doomed, but Hitler unaccountably held off for two days. The Allies were able to reach the coast and seal off a defensive perimeter around Dunkirk.

A French tank gunner surrenders to German infantrymen. A shell had hit the French tank and killed the rest of the crew; the gunner could not drive.

A German squad carries out a textbook assault on an Allied fortified bunker. The chief weapon was the hand grenade, which caused the defenders to close the bunker's ports, blinding them. Then the trapped enemy was bombed with grenades dropped through gun slits.

An invader rides across France with a French flag. LIFE, accepting the German caption, said it had been captured in battle, but a reader pointed out that military color would have had a gold fringe; this flag had presumably been liberated from some post office or town hall.

Maintaining formation while waiting for embarkation in the longest queue of their lives, British troops describe an enormous letter "S"

Reprieve at Dunkirk

To officers of the British Expeditionary Force trapped on the beaches at France's northernmost point, the escape plan was known as Operation Dynamo. To the rest of the non-Axis world it came to be known as the Miracle of Dunkirk. It also became a rallying cry and back-stiffener for the beleaguered British nation.

For more than a week the Royal Navy had been preparing for what seemed impossible: the removal of hundreds of thousands of men from a hostile shore with only a small harbor. Destroyers had the most heroic role. They crammed as many soldiers as possible into their limited deck space and raced with them across the strait to Dover, their guns ablaze to protect themselves and other, unarmed craft. But they could not do it alone. Big ships had to lie outside the harbor while smaller boats ferried men to them. When it became evident, on May 29, that small craft were effective, Britons manned everything from yachts to trawlers and joined the action. The R.A.F., meanwhile, stood off the Luftwaffe until more than 338,000 men had been saved, a third of them French.

On the beach, a British soldier shoots back at German planes. "This is pure irritation, has no effect on planes," said LIFE's military expert.

"This shot of Dunkirk ranks as great war art," was LIFE's comment about the picture above of evacuees photographed by one of their number.

on Dunkirk beach. Formations broke up at the waterline, since rescue vessels varied from private launches to warships.

A mass of Tommies wait for places in small boats—like the one at right—that will take them to cross-Channel transportation. In the background is a wrecked, beached ship. Despite casualties from ship sinkings and bombing of the shore, almost all evacuees reached safety.

A joyful Führer 'jigs' on the corpse of the Third Republic

The happiest moment in the life of Adolf Hitler is recorded in a newsreel as the Führer, with his staff, gets the news on June 17, 1940, that France is ready to

'Inconceivable that this gay metropolis should be dead'

When France fell, Louis P. Lochner had been head of the Berlin Bureau of the Associated Press for 12 years. Like all correspondents in Germany he was under a so-called "responsibility" censorship not to write material offensive to the Nazis. The following is part of what he cabled on entering Paris with the Germany Army:

I have passed through many ghost towns in Belgium and northern France since the western offensive began on May 10 but no experience has become more indelibly fixed in my mind than that of entering the French nation's incomparable capital, Paris, on June 14, immediately after the first German vanguard. It seemed inconceivable, even though I stood on the spot, that this teeming, gay, noisy metropolis should be dead. Yet dead it was. It seemed inconceivable that it was in German hands. Yet occupied by Germans it was.

Except for Parisian police standing at street corners there was hardly a soul in this city of over four million. Everybody had fled before Germany's irresistible advance—70 per cent to nearby towns and villages, 30 per cent into the privacy of their homes.

You who have been to Paris, just imagine this picture: at the Place de la Concorde no such merry-go-round of honking autos, screaming news vendors, gesticulating cops, gaily chatting pedestrians as usually characterizes this magnificent square. Instead, depressing silence broken only now and then by the purr of some German officer's motor as it made its way to the Hotel Crillon, headquarters of the hastily set up local German commandery. On the hotel's flagstaff, the swastika fluttered in the breeze where once the Stars and Stripes had been in the days of 1919 when Wilson received the cheers of French crowds from the balcony.

surrender. The widely shown newsreel was a hoax, perpetrated by a Canadian film editor who doctored it to make Hitler "dance."

◄One week after his "victory jig," Hitler parades in Paris with his officers before the Eiffel Tower, symbol of his monumental victory. German troops had entered the city ten days earlier, five days after French Generalissimo Maxime Weygand had warned the government to leave and one day after Paris was declared an open city.

A spectator in Marseilles weeps as he sees a parade of flags of defeated French regiments being sent to Algeria for safekeeping. The picture, taken from a *Movietone News* clip, is controversial; ever since it ran in LIFE, its subject has been variously identified by volunteer researchers as a black marketeer, a uniform manufacturer and an emotional Italian visitor.

1939-1941

Battle of Britain

A powerful German air force poised across the Channel in what had recently been friendly territory gave Britons a severe case of invasion jitters. No enemy had succeeded in invading their island since the Norman Conquest in 1066—but they knew that the airplane could change all that. The British Air Ministry had not been idle, and when Hermann Göring, in August of 1940, launched his all-out campaign to knock out the R.A.F. Fighter Command, under the brilliant Sir Hugh Dowding, he was in for a surprise. Flying the improved Hurricane and brand-new Spitfire fighters, the young (average age 23), dedicated and skillful R.A.F. pilots, many from the Commonwealth nations, met the aerial nemeses of Europe and shot them down. Of these young fighter pilots Churchill made one of his most memorable remarks: "Never in the field of human conflict was so much owed by so many to so few." Pressing too hard for victory, Göring switched his attacks from R.A.F. air fields, a tactic that might have won him the Battle of Britain in another two weeks, to London and civilian targets. He had lost the battle by the end of September.

Antiaircraft gunner

With more curiosity than fear, children of English hop pickers watch from a ditch as R.A.F. and Luftwaffe fighters engage in a dogfight.

St. Paul's Cathedral, rebuilt after the 1666 London fire, miraculously survived the 10,000-bomb fire raid of December 29, 1940.

England under the Blitz: some of the greatest heroes were the

LIFE

AIR-RAID VICTIM

SEPTEMBER 23, 1940 **10** CENTS
YEARLY SUBSCRIPTION $4.50

HELP !

DEFEND AMERICA
BY AID TO BRITAIN
WM. ALLEN WHITE COMMITTEE

A victim of the Luftwaffe named Eileen Dunne peers forlornly from a
LIFE cover at the height of the
bombing of Britain. The photograph
was one of a number of pictures of
bomb devastation in northern England that were sent to the magazine
by the society photographer Cecil
Beaton. Two months later, both it
and a similar picture of another
wounded child *(right and opposite),*
by William Vandivert, had been
turned into war posters in the U.S.

STOP THIS !

HELP BRITAIN
STOP HITLER

COMMITTEE TO DEFEND AMERICA BY AIDING THE ALLIES

Frederick Harrison, 6, stands with
sister Winnie, 3, whom he saved,
along with his mother and the baby,
when their London home was hit. He

smallest

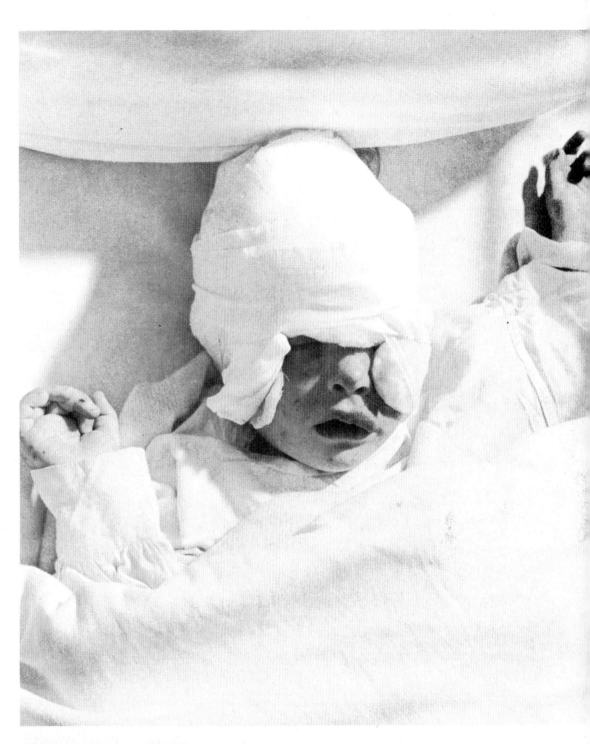

was buried in rubble but burrowed his way out, pulled away the debris that pinned down his sisters, then led a search for their mother.

"Margaret Curtis, 2," LIFE said under the picture above in its September 9, 1940, issue, "is about to die." Her mother, shielding Margaret with her own body from a German bomb, had been killed, as had Margaret's father and grandmother.

A year later a friend of the Curtises' wrote LIFE that Margaret was alive (left) but stricken dumb, and that her mother was alive too. That letter caused American neurosurgeon Dr. Henry L. Heyl in London to ask the magazine for help in locating the child for possible treatment. When she was found, it was learned that it was her brother Royston, 7, who was the speechless one. The doctor performed two delicate brain operations, and Royston talked again.

German bombers unite a class-ridden nation in its finest hour

Symbol of the English doggedness that frustrated Hitler, a Trafalgar Square vendor warms her hands over a dying fire bomb. The picture is by William Vandivert, who with others of the LIFE and *Time* staffs survived the blitz. An estimated 48,000 Londoners were killed or wounded.

▲ Eyes closed to a rag-tag regiment of her Women's Mechanized Transport Training Corps, Commandant G. M. Cook salutes. "Doubtless the last straw," LIFE said, "will be the discovery that somebody left a thumb print on the negative, producing the smudge on her greatcoat."

The menace of invasion arouses every Englishman

The Reverend Dr. Jocelyn Henry Temple Perkins, 70, Sacristan and Minor Canon of Westminster Abbey, learns to present arms. In case of invasion, the Canon, an author and a lover of music, travel, architecture and cycling, was prepared to help guard factories and patrol roads.

▲ Civilians, many of them total strangers to firearms, train for the defense of their Kent countryside by popping at clay pigeons, stand-ins for expected Nazi parachutists. Their rifles had been standard issue about 1900. LIFE predicted many of them would shoot one another.

In an anti-subversion drill, a "Nazi fifth columnist" disguised as a nanny "fires on" a Home Guard sentry who was asked for identification.

Taking cover in crane buckets, Home Guards practice defense. For a while, home-front drills were Britain's most ▼ popular activity.

A gaggle of geese waddles past an ▲ antitank unit. With the front lines now in England, photographers got great mileage out of such scenes.

"Wounded" in a civil-defense drill, Londoners act their parts to the satisfaction of CD officials. The British came to call this the Bore War. ▼

Britons take a defiant breather as the invasion threat recedes

▲ Ignoring bombed-out houses and occasionally ducking bombers, the Aldenham Hunt, led by Major Sir Jocelyn Morton Lucas, rides after hare.

Girls in prewar bathing suits enjoy the sun at a seaside resort in 1941, transforming the beach from a front line to an off-duty festival.

The Battle of Britain and the threat of invasion largely ended, a workwoman puts up road signs that had been taken down to baffle paratroops.

British kids turn a bomb crater into a velodrome. Other bomb holes were used as sunken gardens and impromptu swimming pools.

1939-1941

Eastern aggressor

Continuing Horror in China

In Asia, a war even more terrible in death and destruction than the European conflict was entering its fifth year. To drive this point home, LIFE, in its issue of July 28, 1941, followed the picture of English bathing girls on a day off *(previous page)* with the scene of horror at right. The picture was taken in the mountain-girt city of Chungking, deep in the interior, where Chiang Kai-shek's Nationalist government was carrying on the fight with the uneasy cooperation of the Communists and a trickle of supplies coming east from India. Because China was far away and its population enormous, LIFE said, its war got little attention in the U.S. press. But occasionally that distant conflict produced pictures that for sheer terror matched any-

thing out of Europe. The smoke-shrouded scene below was Chungking, the date June 28, 1940, the occasion a Japanese air raid—three hours of high-explosive bombing by 86 planes.

A year later, on June 5, 1941, a raid created the carnage at right through a particularly gruesome sequence of events. The bombers drove 5,000 civilians into Chungking's largest air-raid shelter, a one-and-a-half-mile tunnel. As they were emerging at the all-clear they got warning of another raid and started to push back in, against the press of those headed out. The shelter gates were slammed shut and, for the first time in Chungking, panic broke out. When the gates were opened, 4,000 had been crushed to death or suffocated.

Mountains of smoke and dust rise over the wood and plaster buildings of Chungking's Old City, its stair-step streets filled with dead and wounded. Some 100 shops and 1,000 buildings were damaged in this raid, including schools, hospitals, U.S. missions and the British embassy.

The bodies of entire families lie at the entrance to Chungking's tunnel air-raid shelter, trampled in a stampede flight from a raid. More than $1.4 million in Chinese money and 200 ounces of gold were removed from the bodies; some of it, LIFE said, had been taken by looters.

Waking Giant: New U.S. Tanks and Talent

On the way out

Nowhere was the modernization and expansion of the nation's fighting might more dramatically apparent than in the development of U.S. armored forces, accompanied by the phasing out of mounted cavalry. Until the summer of 1940, U.S. armor had consisted of 400 obsolescent tanks, poorly armored and deficient in firepower. One year later the Army was able to field four armored divisions, each equipped with 385 up-to-date tanks—though the 10-ton light tank below was armed only with machine guns—and 1,900 other vehicles.

A special issue had a cover that featured Second Armored Division Commander Major General George S. Patton Jr., an apostle of armor who was then little known, pictured in his personal tank. For the same issue, LIFE sent photographer-reporter teams out to investigate the state of America's preparedness, and printed pictures of a sham battle at Fort Benning, where Patton was in charge. The issue acknowledged that Patton's assessment of his Second Division ("The strongest force ever devised by man") might be overstated, but calculated that "even to military observers, it seems just as self-sufficient as a Panzer division."

A simulated tank encounter reaches a spectacular climax as a light-tank roars out of the smoke and dust with infantrymen following closely in support. At this point the main body of tanks had penetrated "enemy" positions and seized strongpoints. The mission of the tank-infantry team was to clean up final resistance and take prisoners.

Fascinated with military gadgets, LIFE commissioned this cutaway drawing of the U.S. Army's light tank, slender backbone of the armed forces' combat power. Thirteen feet long, 8 feet wide and 7 feet high, it ran 35 mph on the road, driven by a 235-hp aircraft-type radial engine that filled the interior with racket and made oral communication impossible. Steering levers controlled each track separately, enabling the vehicle to spin 360°.

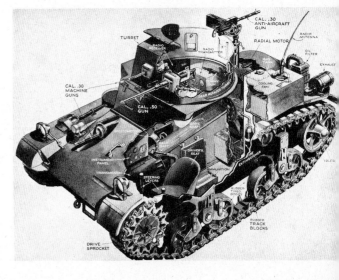

LIFE

DEFENSE ISSUE

U.S. ARMS

JULY 7, 1941 **10** CENTS
YEARLY SUBSCRIPTION $4.50

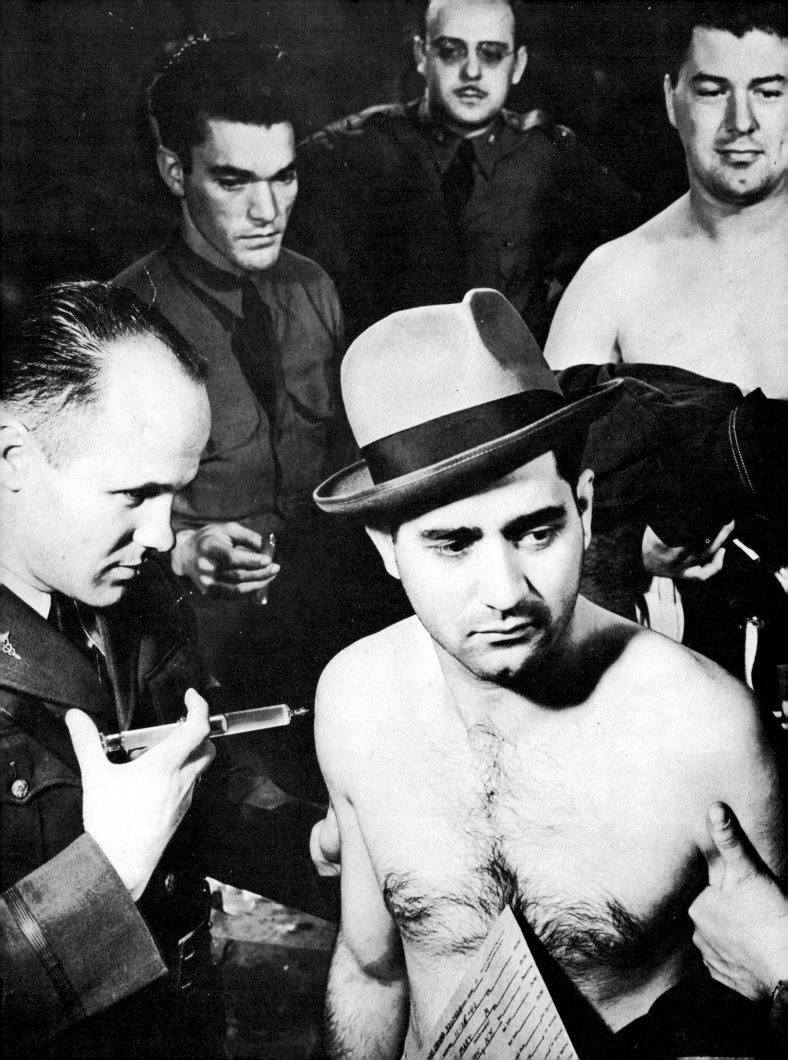

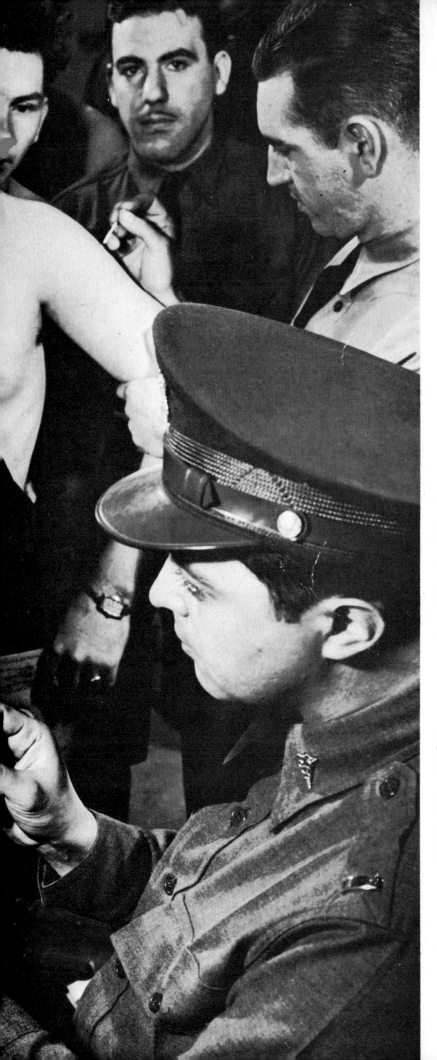

1939-1941
F.D.R. sends 'Greeting'

Although U.S. isolationists remained as vociferous as ever, the fall of France posed the threat of a Germany that might require much more American muscle. To reinforce offshore defenses, Army and Navy air bases were built in Bermuda. But the specter of an Atlantic opened to the German navy by a possible British defeat spurred Congress to give Franklin D. Roosevelt the first peacetime conscription bill in the nation's history. For his part, F. D. R. had been methodically trying to steer a hesitant America toward war with Germany, although he denied any such intent as he ran for his third Presidential term. In midcampaign, Roosevelt signed the Burke-Wadsworth Selective Service Act into law, and one month later more than 16 million men who had passed their 21st birthday, but had not yet passed their 36th, became liable for a year's military duty. On October 29, 1940, numbers drawn from a glass bowl in Washington determined which 900,000 of the registered men would receive the first of those memorable pieces of government mail that began with the fateful word: "Greeting."

By the end of November the President had won his election over Republican Wendell L. Willkie and the first conscripts had marched into some 29 training camps across the country—to raucous cries from Regular Army personnel of "Hello, suckers!"—and received their first inoculations as old timers hooted the warning, "Watch the hook!"

"America's answer to Hitlerism" LIFE called Roosevelt's signing of the draft bill at 3:08 p.m. EST on September 16, 1940.

In George Strock's eloquent picture, draftee Sam Arcadipan gets his smallpox vaccination and typhoid shots from doctors at Fort Dix.

GIs Frank Doolin *(left)* and Forest
Hunter, at Camp Shelby, Mississippi,
illustrate the axiom that there are two
Army sizes: too large and too small.

Butch, the one-month-old pet of a ▶
First Division battery on maneuvers,
stands watchdog duty for his masters'
155mm howitzer during a break.

Battle for an Atlantic Lifeline

The German Navy, using Atlantic bases on the coast of conquered France, preyed on British shipping with increasing success. Its hunting pack included a new class of fast and heavily armed "pocket battleships" of only 10,000 tons, such as the *Deutschland (left)*, but it did far more damage with its old standbys, U-boats and civilian-disguised raiders like Count Felix von Luckner's *Sea Wolf* of World War I fame.

As losses grew, the British kept changing convoy routes and devising new escort techniques, and in March 1941, Churchill proclaimed a full-fledged Battle of the Atlantic. In this phase of the war at sea, one of the disguised German raiders sank a neutral ship, the Egyptian-flag *Zamzam*, sailing from Recife, Brazil, to Capetown with 138 Americans among its 202 passengers. (One of the Americans was a LIFE photographer who shot pictures of the raider and managed to smuggle them out of Europe.) Soon afterward, an American freighter headed for South Africa was sunk by a U-boat. That July the U.S. started building escort vessels for the British and convoying ships between the U.S. and Iceland. On the sea, at least, America was at undeclared war with Germany.

Pocket battleship

Atlantic nemesis

A lifeboat leaves the *Zamzam* after its shelling. The picture, like the one at left, was taken from another boat by LIFE's David Scherman, who had been Africa-bound on assignment.

The raider *Atlantis*, disguised as a freighter named *Tamesis* and carrying three guns, closes in cautiously before picking up lifeboat passengers. Thanks to the appearance of this picture in LIFE, the *Atlantis* was recognized and sunk a few months later by a British cruiser.

A British freighter, photographed with the help of a telescopic lens from the U-boat that torpedoed her, sinks, bow last, into the Atlantic.

The German Navy rescues a game enemy at sea — and vice versa

Survivors of the British destroyer *Glowworm*, coated and half-blinded by their sunken vessel's fuel oil, are hauled out of the North Sea by the crew of one of the German warships that caught her on a mining mission. LIFE called the German photographs of the 1940 sinking and rescue "the greatest pictures yet to come out of this war."

A year later it ran a perfect turnabout photograph—of German sailors of the battleship *Bismarck* being rescued, also in the North Atlantic, by the British heavy cruiser *Dorsetshire*. She had fired the torpedo that finished off the trapped but stubbornly resisting dreadnought.

Survivors' story: a 23-day Atlantic ordeal in an open boat

This is the story told to a LIFE reporter in Brazil by survivors, British and Indian, of the liner Britannia, *sunk by a German raider, after 38 of them had staggered ashore following 23 days in a lifeboat:*

Our lifeboat, built to hold 50, had 82 men. We took turns squatting and standing up. The wounded were placed at the bottom of the boat, but two inches of water leaked into the bottom and some of the wounded drowned when their faces were pressed into the bilge by the crowd.

During the first week we saw eight ships. We shouted and burned oil so that they might see the smoke. None did. When it rained one day, we filled three buckets with drinking water.

For the next 16 days we sailed the South Atlantic. The heat nearly crazed us and the glare closed our eyes until they were slits. Each morning we dumped overboard the men who had died the night before. At first we buried them with a short religious service, but later we were too weak to do even this.

By the third week men began losing their minds. An Englishman named Smith screamed deliriously for his wife until he died. Those with strength left tried to bail out the boat and clean up the vomit of the seasick men. For food we had a daily ration of one cracker and a spoonful of condensed milk mixed with water. Some of the men fought for the leftover cracker scraps. Our mouths cracked from dryness.

After two weeks of sunshine it rained again. We spread sails out to catch the rain and we opened our mouths to let the rain fall in. In desperation, however, two Hindus drank salt water and later jumped overboard. We were too weak to rescue them.

On the 19th day the color of the water changed and strands of seaweed floated by. Land could not be far away, but three more men died that day. By now there was much more room in which to sprawl out, but the legs of some of the men had become so numb from sitting that they could not move over.

On the 23rd day we sighted land! When our navigator saw it, he mumbled: "I have done my duty. You are all safe." Then he collapsed and died.

Later that day we landed at low tide. Many of the men could no longer walk or talk. They simply collapsed in the mud. The others stumbled farther ashore, bowing their heads to thank God for deliverance. If these men had not awakened in time that night, the weaker men, lying in the mud, would have drowned beneath the incoming tide. Shortly after the weaker men had been dragged to safety, we heard human voices. At the sight of the Brazilian fishermen who found us, some of us fainted with happiness.

Safe in Brazil, the English survivors of the sinking of the *Britannia* still appear numbed by their ordeal, despite a few brave attempts at smiles.

Infantrymen of the Panzer force leave the protection of their armored troop carriers to rush a farmhouse that is sheltering Russian sharp-shooters. Russia's "scorched-earth" policy left the advancing Nazis few unburned buildings, like the one below being taken by the riflemen. Rising out of its own dust cloud, a German armored assault gun races down a dirt road. The Nazis' most ▼ effective weapon on Russia's vast plains, this vehicle carried slabs of armor heavier than a tank's and a 105mm howitzer with which it could knock out pillboxes point-blank.

Attack on Russia

On the second day of the summer of 1941, Nazi Germany converted the Soviet Union from partner to enemy. In his grandiose plan, code-named Barbarossa (for Frederick I, known as Barbarossa, or Redbeard), Hitler proposed to crush the Red Army in a month. And in the opening days of "the biggest battle in the history of the world," it looked as if he might. As more than five million men in German gray-green and Red Army khaki struggled for the Ukraine and the Baltic steppingstones to Leningrad, the Nazi combat pictures looked much like those from Poland and France. Spearheaded by armored groups, the Germans advanced 50 miles toward Leningrad, whose capture would enable them to supply their troops by ship. In 18 days they were in Leningrad province, and on July 10 their pincer movement had closed on Minsk, taken the city and captured 300,000 prisoners.

But this was not the usual blitzkrieg. The Red Army soldiers, unlike the Nazis, had been taught to fight as individuals. They were skilled guerrillas and they had a vast country at their backs. The German radio admitted: "This war is not much like Poland or France. Almost everywhere in our rear violent fighting flares up continuously. All is in flux." A rearming America and a hard-pressed Britain took heart—and the usually xenophobic Russians soon recognized that they were standard-bearers in a common cause.

German riflemen (dangerously close together, LIFE pointed out) fire at Russian snipers guarding an antitank
▼ emplacement in western Russia.

In the map above, reprinted from LIFE, July 7, 1941, dark arrows show the main thrusts of German forces invading Russia. The arrow pointing north was aimed at Leningrad, Russia's second city. In the south a pincer movement drove at Minsk, key rail junction for Moscow.

A press convoy sinks in Russia's S[e]ptember mud. The weather, plus R[us]sian valor spurred by scenes [like] those shown here, stalled the Na[zis.] The autumn rains were the heav[iest] in the memory of living Russians[.]

◄ The bodies of five ununiformed R[us]sians—executed by the Germans [for] not fighting according to "inter[na]tional law"—hang from a gibbet i[n a] field near Smolensk. The photogra[ph] was found on the body of a d[ead] German officer.

A Russian and his wife mourn th[eir] son, whose body they have disco[v]ered among other guerrillas execu[ted] by the German invaders. "Multip[ly] the picture 10,000,000 times," sa[id] LIFE, "and you will get some idea [of] family anguish in Russia, where [a] war is being fought in every hom[e."]

Old salts Franklin Roosevelt and Winston Churchill sit before their staffs (including, at right, staff chiefs General George C. Marshall and General Sir John G. Dill) on the deck of H.M.S. *Prince of Wales.* LIFE pointed out that where Hitler and Mussolini had held "ineffable conclaves" on an armored train in the Brenner Pass, "the leaders of the two great English-speaking democracies met upon the clean windy sea." It also observed that the P.M., "wearing the nondescript naval uniform he always affects at sea, looked rather like a well-to-do tugboat captain."

Leader in a new role

The Triple Alliance

Two meetings within two weeks in midsummer 1941 marked the beginning of the potent alliance of the Big Three. On July 28 and 31, Franklin Roosevelt's "eyes and ears," Presidential assistant Harry Hopkins, met with Joseph Stalin in the Kremlin to find out for F.D.R. the extent of the Russian war effort and what the Premier needed from the U.S. in order to fight the Germans. His findings were: a driving Russian war plan on a colossal scale and a $1 billion shopping list of war matériel.

Then, on August 9, President Roosevelt held the first of nine meetings—code-named Argentia—with Winston Churchill on the U.S. cruiser *Augusta* and the British battleship *Prince of Wales* in Placentia Bay, Newfoundland. When the conferences were over, the two issued a joint declaration, called the Atlantic Charter, that summarized the war aims of their peoples. It also reinforced a warm personal relationship that would help forge the Anglo-American war effort. Significantly, the meeting was followed with an invitation to Stalin (Churchill had said he would make a pact with the devil to defeat Hitler) to make it a threesome. Stalin quickly accepted.

U.S. envoy Hopkins and Stalin pose stiffly for LIFE's Margaret Bourke-White. Hopkins played errandboy and brought her films to the U.S.

Oldtime patriotism overflows to help an ally

Workers at a Philadelphia plant opened by Disston, a tool company to make armor plate celebrate by creating a sea of flags. The picture opened a special issue of LIFE titled "The Arming of America."

A creative chef (*far left*) exhibits a patriotic dish at the 72nd Annual Salon of Culinary Art in New York. The flag flowers were wax; the turkey was edible. Roll upon roll of U.S. flags (*left*) are printed at Annin & Co., America's foremost flagmaker. Patriotism caused the biggest flag boom since 1917, and Annin expected to sell 16 million in 1940.

Patriotism in the U.S. extended to help for Britain. New York society's William Rhinelander Stewart plucks a $10 star from stripper Gypsy Rose Lee at a British War Relief ball.

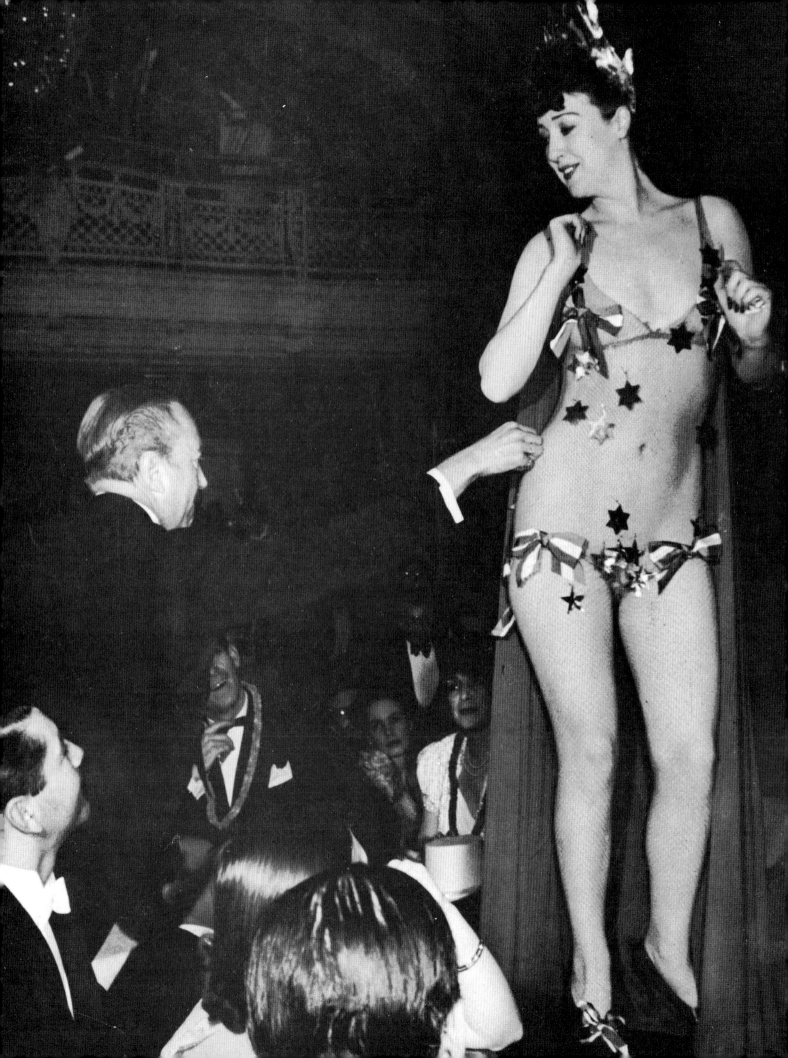

An Imperial Wedding and a Royal Double Cross

The issue of LIFE dated December 8, 1941, contained not a word about the principal event of that week. But the issue did lead off with the picture below, captioned so that it later struck a lot of readers as a journalistic coup—clear evidence that LIFE's editors had known about aggressive Japanese plans in advance of what later occurred.

Not so. The issue had gone to press one day too early to catch the big news, which the editors had foreseen no better than anyone else. They had, however, been keeping track of the worsening relations between the U.S. and Japan. The previous issue had shown the picture at right of Hirohito's two envoys in Washington, where they were ostensibly trying to patch things up. To keep the story running, LIFE played a royal Japanese wedding picture big, and accompanied it by comments about a warlike Japan—summed up in what seemed the product of a crystal ball: "The stage is set for war."

For his pre-Pearl Harbor wedding to Yuriko Takagi, a viscount's daughter, Prince Mikasa, the Japanese emperor's youngest brother, holds a scepter and wears a lacquered hat. Both accoutrements had been part of traditional formal garb in Japan since 1000 A.D.

Special Envoy Saburo Kurusu (left) and Japanese Ambassador Kichisaburo Nomura grin for a photographer at the Department of State. The two met with President Roosevelt ▶ and Secretary of State Cordell Hull, seeking to persuade the U.S. to cease helping China and Russia.

1942

Stars and stripes

New recruit

Flying Fortress

U-boat spotter

Coastal defense

Silent assault team

Freighters' weaponry

Furlough fun

Outdoor assembly line

1943

Military millinery

Cold-weather warrior

Marine fighter hero

Escort fighter

Needle worker

Egyptian front

III. TURNING POINT

The Axis thrust hits an Allied roadblock

For the first five months after Pearl Harbor, Japan owned the Pacific. With all the U.S. Pacific Fleet's battleships sunk in the mud of Pearl Harbor, Guam and Wake, Hong Kong and Singapore fell. Thailand was overrun. Burma was lost—and with it land access to China. Americans thirsted for word of some retribution, but the news kept getting worse; the Netherlands East Indies succumbed, and the Japanese attacked Australia itself. Then the U.S. lost the Philippines after a costly and demoralizing stand against overwhelming odds. With these island conquests, the Japanese planned to set up a girdle of defense that would enable them to exploit the oil and raw-material riches of Malaya and the East Indies, Japan's so-called "Greater East Asia Co-Prosperity Sphere."

The means to fight back were still scanty. President Roosevelt called for 60,000 planes, but even the "arsenal of democracy" would require some time to reach that goal. Under prior agreements reached between F. D. R. and Churchill, naval strength could not be diverted from the war against Hitler. And there the news was equally gloomy. The Russians were still barely holding their scorched and frozen earth; General Erwin Rommel's Afrika Korps was moving in North Africa as the Italians never had.

But there were auguries of better news to come. Hitler was fighting a war on two fronts, a nightmare he had sworn to avoid. Winter Fritz, as the German infantryman in the snowy vastness of the eastern front was called, was dying in huge numbers. Almost overnight naval warfare had undergone the change General Billy Mitchell had predicted in 1920: Japanese bombers and torpedo planes had sunk His Majesty's heavy cruiser *Repulse* and battleship *Prince of Wales.* No longer would such floating gun platforms decide naval engagements. The carrier was the new queen of the fleet and all three U.S. Pacific carriers, which had been out on maneuvers on December 7 (with LIFE photographer Bob Landry), were in operation. Before midyear 1942, the carriers struck back. In the Coral Sea the Japanese fleet,

attempting to reinforce New Guinea, recoiled after a standoff; at Midway the Japanese Navy suffered its first decisive defeat. From that moment on, the Pacific war went the other way.

The Marines landed on Guadalcanal and MacArthur's Yanks and Aussies turned the Japanese around on New Guinea, opening the way for reconquest of the Pacific. A turn-around could also be seen in the war against Hitler. Lieutenant General Bernard Montgomery routed the overextended Rommel at El Alamein, and the Americans landed in North Africa, an operation code-named Torch that Churchill called, along with the rest of the turn-around, the "end of the beginning." Stalingrad, a supposed walk-over for the Nazis, turned into a debacle; 22 German divisions trapped there in November were reduced to eating their horses before Field Marshal Friedrich Paulus defied Hitler's orders in January and surrendered.

LIFE had shifted into war gear with no discernible disruption. Indeed, it had been in basic training for two years before Pearl Harbor. Its photographers and combat artists were already at the fronts. The Modern Living section became War Living. Virtually every article—on education, religion, science, fashions, even art—was "war-angled," mined for its relation to the war effort. A succession of practical manuals helped the readers adjust to scarcities and sacrifice: How to Grow a Victory Garden, How to Buy a Horse (to save fuel), How to Make Coffee (to save coffee), How to Knit. When Henry Kaiser built a Liberty ship in a record ten days, LIFE even explained How to Weld.

But nuts and bolts were only a small part of the history that was in the making. The magazine recognized an incubating legend when a Navy chaplain inspired Private Frank Loesser to write "Praise the Lord and Pass the Ammunition." LIFE called it the "first indigenous spontaneous song" of World War II and ran Chaplain William Maguire's picture on the cover. But the tear-jerking line that spoke to GIs everywhere that year came from an Irving Berlin song that Bing Crosby introduced. It went: "I'm dreaming of a white Christmas. . ."

On the anniversary of Pearl Harbor, the headline on LIFE's lead story read "The Allies Launch World Offensive." The article said that "on every world front except China, Germany and its allies were in retreat," and noted that Goebbels was "frantically recalling copies" of a Nazi film called *The Victory in Africa.* In the desert, the graves with the Iron Crosses were no longer marked, "He Died for Hitler." Now they read, "He Died for Germany."

1942-1943

DECEMBER 22, 1941 10 CENTS
YEARLY SUBSCRIPTION $4.50

Old Glory challenged

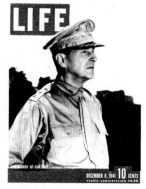

COMMANDER OF FAR EAST
DECEMBER 8, 1941 10 CENTS
YEARLY SUBSCRIPTION $4.50

Old soldier MacArthur

The Sneak Attack

On December 7, 1941, planes from six Japanese aircraft carriers sank six American battleships at Pearl Harbor, Hawaii, destroyed 164 U.S. planes on the ground and killed five times as many sailors (2,008) as had died in World War I. The Japanese planes, spotted on Army radar, were dismissed as a "mistake," and were not reported until too late.

On LIFE's cover that week was a picture of General Douglas MacArthur, "Commander of the Far East," and inside was a wedding portrait of Emperor Hirohito's brother *(page 104)*. But these signs that LIFE was abreast of the news were fortuitous. For its next two issues censorship confined the magazine to peacetime pictures of Pearl Harbor and an artist's rendition of the attack. (The picture opposite did not appear for another year.) But the editors made up for a lack of pictures by colorful prose. A lead article *(below)* castigated Japan for committing "national hara-kiri."

As nothing else could have, the sneak attack galvanized an America that was by no means ready for war. It would be a while before charges were leveled that F.D.R., wanting to bring the crisis to a head, had known about the attack in advance. For the moment, the country was united as it had never been before.

With a bold newspaper-style headline, LIFE declares war on Japan, which attacked Pearl Harbor without "even such an ultimatum as Hitler is wont to send while his legions pour across some new border."

The battleship *West Virginia*, her decks awash, sinks alongside her mooring shortly after being struck by Japanese torpedoes at Pearl Harbor.

Overnight, Americans unite to work, save and do without

The commandant of the Brooklyn Navy Yard presides over a send-off for workers who volunteered to go to Pearl Harbor to salvage and repair the wrecked American men-of-war.

The last civilian car built in the U.S.—a gray Pontiac—rolls off the production line on February 2, 1942. Thereafter, automobile plants were used to produce planes, tanks and other war matériel.

Thousands of new and used tires are piled 40 feet deep in a B. F. Goodrich yard in Akron, Ohio. Within weeks after Pearl Harbor, the sale of new tires was banned and old tires were collected from junkyards. A shortage of rubber, produced in the threatened East Indies, was the single largest factor in keeping U.S. cars off the highways.

The 'arsenal of democracy' begins pumping out a flow of arms

and men

Launched sideways in limited space, the flag-and-bunting decorated submarine *Peto* smites the water at a shipyard in Manitowoc, Wisconsin.

Heavyweight champ Joe Louis, bundled up against the chill at Camp Upton, Long Island, in 1942, shoulders arms as a $21-a-month recruit.

Japanese Juggernaut in the East

Singapore's Commander

While the cleanup was still going on at Pearl Harbor, Japanese forces struck with stunning swiftness across thousands of miles of ocean, dismantling Asian empires that had taken the British and Dutch centuries to build. In a matter of weeks, they took Hong Kong, the Philippines, Burma, Borneo and Java; their soldiers entered Bangkok, capital of neutral Thailand, without a fight. By January 1942, Japanese planes were raiding the Australian bastion on Rabaul in the South Pacific, and in an audacious attack had wrecked shipping in Darwin, Australia. And the juggernaut kept rolling. In February, the Japanese captured Singapore, astounding the British and leading LIFE to observe that "White men had taken their most catastrophic defeat at the hands of yellow men since the days of Genghis Khan."

The defeat was all the worse for its seeming impossibility. Singapore was the most powerful fortress in Asia, defended by 90,000 crack British troops and protected by batteries of 15-inch guns. Yet this military might was deployed in vain. The Japanese—many of them using bicycles—slipped down the Malay Peninsula and fell upon Singapore from the rear. Since its mighty guns were trained toward the sea and incapable of firing inland, Singapore surrendered within a week.

LIFE photographer Carl Mydans accompanied tropical-uniformed Aussies patrolling the jungle near Singapore before the Japanese invasion.

114

a. Leydenfrost

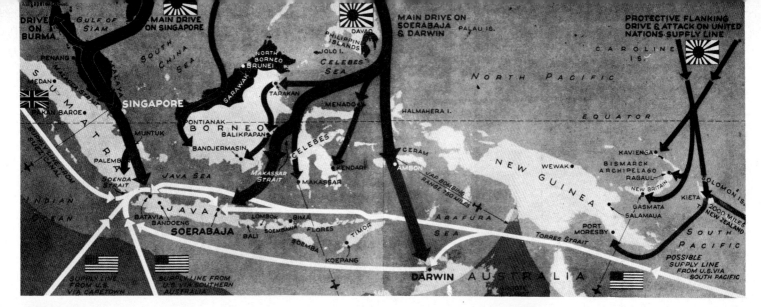

Black arrows on a LIFE map of Asia show how Japanese forces, scattered across the Pacific, seized territory from the Solomon Islands in the east to the Philippines, Burma, Borneo and Singapore in the west. Gray arrows indicate LIFE's speculation—which proved remarkably accurate—about probable Japanese moves that threatened to conquer still more real estate and endanger potential U.S. supply lines in the region.

In a re-creation by LIFE artist Alexander Leydenfrost of Singapore's last hours, Japanese troops clamber ashore at night from shallow-draft armored barges driven by aircraft propellers. Launched on the Malay Peninsula's mainland, the barges crossed the Singapore channel where it was less than half a mile wide. They disgorged men and medium tanks, like the one shown here, against exhausted Australian troops who had been rushed in to defend the city's exposed rear.

Cane in hand, a somber Douglas MacArthur and his Chief of Staff leave the tunnel headquarters on Corregidor shortly before it fell to the Japanese.

1942-1943

With no choice, America abandons its heroes

The weakness of the battered Pacific fleet—compounded by American naval commitments in the Battle of the Atlantic *(pages 158–161)*—meant the inevitable, tragic abandonment of the Philippines in the face of the overwhelming forces that Japan landed there. The "Philippine epic," as LIFE rightly called the doomed but tenacious American stand, was photographed with harrowing effectiveness by Melville Jacoby, who provided the magazine with the photographs of MacArthur *(above)*, the Bataan wounded and the dim bowels of Corregidor, where he wrote his last stories by candlelight *(page 6)*.

Jacoby escaped to Australia and was killed in a freak accident, becoming LIFE's first war casualty.

For the GIs at Corregidor the situation was untenable. Demoralized and near starvation after a 28-day seige, they surrendered. In anger and sadness, LIFE presented what was perhaps the most shocking scene for Americans of the entire war: the famous photograph opposite of the capitulation. "It is a good thing that this kind of taunt returns to slap Americans in the face," said the editors, "for it makes sure that the memory of the defeat will not slide easily from American minds."

Melville Jacoby snapped this picture of Army Medical Corps nurses. It was later duplicated exactly for the film *So Proudly We Hail.*

A Japanese photographer's picture ▶ shows weary, dejected Americans filing out of a Corregidor tunnel with a white flag of surrender.

116

Grinning Japanese guard GIs rounded up at Corregidor as the grimy survivors start on their infamous Death March to prison camps 60 miles away.

'Death was a part of our life'

Not until two years after the fall of Corregidor did the authorities permit the story of what happened subsequently to be released. LIFE printed a detailed account of atrocity, murder and starvation that was inflicted by the Japanese on their American prisoners. It was written by two of a group of 10 men who managed to escape. This is a part of it:

At the end of the day the Japanese usually dispatched those prisoners who seemed so weakened that they would not be able to go on. There were many cases of burial alive, often with the forced assistance of American officers. Some of the prisoners were forced to dig their own graves.

A prisoner told what took place on such occasions: "The first time it happened," he said, "I didn't know what was up. An enlisted man had keeled over—he had been stumbling for hours—and the Japs dragged him out of the line to a ditch about a hundred yards from the road. I was taken out of the line and escorted to where the Japs had placed this unconscious man in the ditch. One of them handed me a shovel. Another jabbed a bayonet into my side and gave an order in Japanese. A Jap grabbed the shovel out of my hands and demonstrated by throwing a few shovelsful of earth on the unconscious soldier. Then he handed me the shovel. God! . . . It doesn't help to tell myself that the soldier, and others later, were already more dead than alive. . . . The worst time was once when a burial victim with about six inches of earth over him suddenly regained consciousness and clawed his way out until he was almost sitting upright. Then I learned to what lengths a man will go to hang onto his own life. The bayonets began to prod me in the side and I was forced to bash the

At bayonet point, Americans had to bury one another alive.

soldier over the head with the shovel and then finish burying him."

The prisoner who told me this story did so several times but he never told it with an excuse for his own conduct. It was unspoken between us that a man already crazed by thirst and hunger, and already at the point of exhaustion, is not a rational being. Automatic reflexes alone will cause him to hang onto his existence with all the remaining life that is in him.

117

Some Good News

After the Philippine disaster, any news that did not spell defeat or humiliation was not merely welcomed by victory-hungry Americans, it was demanded. For weeks the diet was meager—an occasional submarine sinking of enemy ships. Then on April 18, 1942, the Joint Chiefs of Staff mounted an audacious attack against Japan itself when Army Air Force Colonel Jimmy Doolittle led a carrier-launched flight of B-25 bombers against the Japanese capital.

As a quick antidote for bad news, Doolittle's Tokyo raid was spectacularly successful, and was thoroughly exploited for its morale value. LIFE photographer Ralph Morse and correspondent John Field were taken along with Vice-Admiral "Bull" Halsey's carrier force to cover the take-off, and photographs of the actual flight over Japan were released to the press.

Back in the U.S., Doolittle was hailed as a hero and decorated by President Roosevelt. Pressed by newsmen during the initial news blackout to reveal where the raiders had come from, F.D.R. grinned broadly and replied, "Shangri-La," recalling James Hilton's popular novel *Lost Horizon* and providing the name for a future U.S. aircraft carrier.

Two months after Corregidor fell, the Navy released this photograph of a Japanese destroyer taken through the periscope of the sub that sank it.

Air Force chief Hap Arnold and Mrs. Doolittle look on as President Roosevelt pins the Congressional Medal of Honor on the colonel.

'The Japanese towns look like chidren's play gardens'

The following is from LIFE's account of the Tokyo raid by Major John Hilger, Jimmy Doolittle's second-in-command:

I will never forget this day as long as I live. At 4:15 a.m. we were called to battle stations and knew that we would not be released before take-off. Colonel Doolittle, flying the No. 1 plane, got off nicely at 8:20, in spite of the rough weather, which threw sea water over the flight deck. The other planes followed quickly in order. The sailors and men on deck cheered lustily when the colonel got off and I think they really thought it couldn't be done. My plane was to go to Nagoya.

The take-off was not particularly difficult even though the gross load of the plane was more than 25,000 pounds and the deck run available was about 500 feet. The wind over the deck was 45 to 50 mph. Full flap was used and all of us had room left over. Take-off 9:15. When about 70 miles due south of Nagoya we separated and I turned for Nagoya. All of our flight had been at about 100 feet, and we continued on up the east side of Ise Bay at this altitude.

On the outskirts of the city we passed over a park where a large crowd was witnessing a baseball game. They still did not suspect an air raid. It was a beautiful spring day with not a cloud in the sky. The Japanese country is beautiful and their towns look like children's play gardens. It is a shame to bomb them but they asked for it.

As we started our climb to our bombing altitude of 1,500 feet, the antiaircraft opened up on us. I will never forget the hurt and indignant tone in Sergeant

LIFE's Ralph Morse shot Doolittle's B-25 taking off from the *Hornet*.

Bain's voice as he called over the interphone and said, "Major, those guys are shooting at us." The antiaircraft fire was moderately heavy in volume but inaccurate. Only two or three shots were close. The size of the bursts indicated it was from medium caliber (about 40mm) guns. We swung around to the left onto a southerly course and picked up our first target, the military barracks which surround Nagoya Castle, the military headquarters of that district. The first bombs dropped and nicely bracketed the barracks buildings, of which there were about 20. Sergeant Eierman saw many intense fires start among them. I quickly turned toward our second target, an oil and gasoline storage warehouse.

Our third target was an arsenal, a tremendous building with a high, arched roof. We could have hit it with our eyes shut. By this time the air was thick with black puffs of smoke from A.A., and fires were starting on the ground behind us.

Our fourth and last target was one that I had been waiting to take a crack at ever since this war started. It was the Mitsubishi Aircraft Works. We hit it dead center. If there is anything in that

building that is inflammable, it is probably still burning.

We dropped down almost to the water and flew due south. When we were 30 miles from Nagoya, we looked back and saw a huge column of oily black smoke standing over the city. Our bombs had started their work. We picked up a terrific tail wind, and for the first time since morning, knew that we had a chance of seeing the night out. We were all pleased and proud of the success of our bombing but now we were like a bunch of kids for we knew we had a chance to live long enough to tell about it.

Just at dark and about one hour off the China Coast we ran into zero-zero weather and went on instruments. I had little premonition then of what was waiting for us. At 1920 (Chungking time) we estimated that we were over our objective in unoccupied China, and I gave the order to bail out. I've never been as lonesome in my life as I was when I looked back and found I was all alone in the plane. I trimmed the plane for level flight and slid my seat back to get out. I sat down on the edge of the escape hatch, leaned over and let go.

Its crew bailed out, Doolittle's plane crashed in China.

The Tables Turned: Coral Sea and Midway

The battles of Coral Sea and Midway marked the turning point in the Pacific war and also a revolution in naval warfare. For the first time major sea engagements were waged primarily by carrier-borne planes. Coral Sea began on May 4, 1942, when planes from U.S. carriers attacked a Japanese invasion convoy heading for New Guinea and sank 14 ships. Three days later, Japanese and American carrier planes attacked one another's flattops. In the action a Japanese destroyer and the light carrier *Shoho* were sunk, and the fleet carriers *Zuikaku* and *Shokaku* were badly damaged. The Japanese clobbered the U.S. carrier *Yorktown* and crippled the *Lexington*, but they were so mauled they had to abandon their invasion plans.

LIFE re-created the scene with photographs of models built by Norman Bel Geddes.

Stung but hardly beaten, fleet commander Isoroku Yamamoto sailed eastward less than a month later with a huge task force built around five carriers. He planned to lure the Americans into battle by attacking the U.S. base at Midway, then crush the U.S. Pacific fleet with his superior one. But the U.S. Navy had broken the Japanese code. Arriving at Midway first, U.S. carriers launched aircraft that pounced on the unsuspecting Japanese fleet, sinking four of five carriers, and inflicting upon Japan its first naval defeat since 1870. From that point on in World War II, Japan was on the defensive.

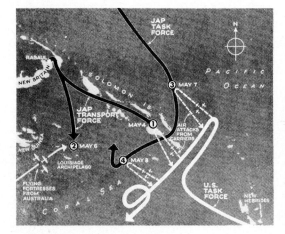

In this map of the Coral Sea battle, dark arrows trace Japanese movements, light arrows U.S. maneuvers. Broken lines show air attacks.

Explosions of aviation fuel from belowdecks gas lines shake the *Lexington*. The *Lex* had already been ripped by two Japanese torpedoes.

Bel Geddes' model ships, viewed through the simulated bubble of a bomber, zigzag in a vivid re-creation of the attack that knocked out the Japanese light carrier *Shoho (center)*.

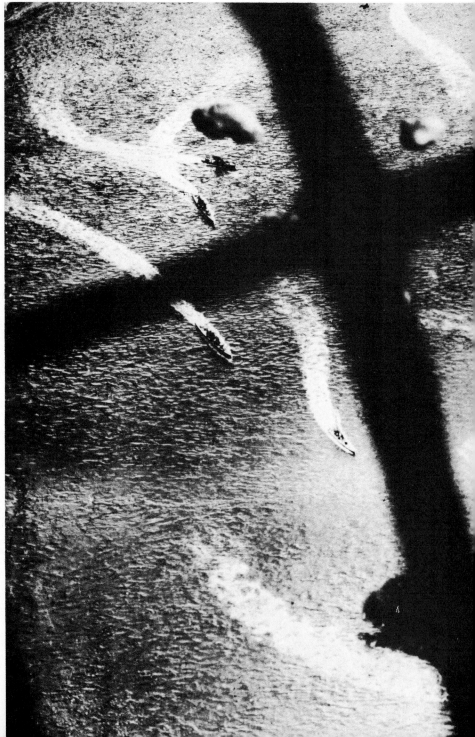

Crewmen of the wounded *Lexington* scramble down ropes as a smoke-shrouded destroyer pulls alongside to pick up survivors.

A flight of U.S. dive bombers roars over bright Pacific coral reefs. Aircraft like these sank four carriers in the Battle of Midway, effectively breaking the back of Japanese naval power in the Central Pacific.

A smoldering hulk is all that is left of the heavy cruiser *Mikuma* after being struck by American bombs at Midway. As evidence of U.S. naval might, this picture was reprinted in American publications throughout the war.

Squadron 8's sole survivor.

An epic tale of sacrifice came out of the Battle of Midway

The story of the officers and men of Torpedo Squadron Eight, who located the Japanese fleet at Midway, radioed word back, then attacked without hope of survival, touched the world. Following is a portion of the account Ensign George Gay, the only man out of 30 to return, gave to LIFE's Sidney L. James.

Now there was only Gay's plane left. There was "only one plane left to make a final run-in." Tex Gay doesn't remember whether at the moment the Skipper's message actually flooded through his mind again, but he had seen the Skipper die and he was determined "to go in and get a hit."

Then the voice of Radioman Bob Huntington came into his ears over the intercom from the rear seat. "They got me," it said. "Are you hurt bad?" asked Gay. "Can you move?" There was no answer. Tex took his eyes off the waves long enough to see that Huntington was lifeless, his head limp against the cockpit. As he turned back, he felt a stab in his upper left arm. The hole in his jacket sleeve told him what had happened. He shifted the stick to his left hand, ripped his sleeve, pressed a machine-gun slug from the wound with his thumb. It seemed like something worth saving, so he sought to put it in the pocket of his jacket. When he found his pocket openings held shut by his safety belt and parachute straps and life jacket, he popped it into his mouth.

He kicked his rudder to make his plane slip and skid so as to avoid the Zeros. He was heading straight for the carrier that the Skipper had picked out. The ship turned hard to starboard, seeking to put its bow forward and avoid his torpedo. He swung to the right and aimed for the port bow, about a quarter length back. When he pushed the button to release his torpedo nothing happened. Apparently the electrical releasing equipment had been knocked out. Since his left arm was practically useless from the bullet and a shrapnel wound in his hand, he held the stick between his knees and released the torpedo with the emergency lever. By now he was only 800 yards from the ship and close to the water. He managed to execute a flipper, turning past the bridge of the carrier and clearing the bow by about 10 feet. As he passed over the flight deck he saw Jap crewmen running in all directions to avoid his crashing plane. He zoomed up and over but as he sought to turn back, four Zeros dived on him. An explosive bullet knocked out his left rudder pedal and he careened into the sea, a quarter of a mile from the carrier.

The impact slammed his hood shut tightly and the plane began to sink. He opened the hood and rose to the surface. As he reached the surface, he heard the explosion of his torpedo striking home on the Jap carrier. Floating beside him was a black rubber seat cushion and a deflated rubber boat. Apparently the enemy bullets had broken the straps which held them secure. Afraid that the Zeros would dive again and machine-gun him, Tex held the seat cushion over his head. Two cruisers steamed close by him and a destroyer all but ran him down. The white-clad sailors on the destroyer saw him and ran to the deckside to point him out. However, he was unmolested.

In about ten minutes the dive bombers from his carrier, apprised of the enemy fleet's location by the Skipper's contact report, swooped in. As they exhausted their bomb loads, more came in. The Japanese fleet was in utter confusion, with most of its air arm trapped on the decks of the carriers where they had been refueling. For two hours the bombers dived, sending their destructive loads into ship after ship.

Thus, with all of its 15 planes destroyed and all but one of its pilots killed in its first engagement, Torpedo Squadron Eight had done its part to rout, for the first time in the war, a Japanese fleet. It had also kept the planes which were refueling on the carrier's deck from taking off in time to meet the attack. Had the Skipper not played his hunch with his faithful boys following in his wake, the planes that were caught refueling on the decks of the Jap carriers might have had time to take the air again to reverse the tide of battle.

When the next dawn came, the ships of the enemy fleet that had not sunk had limped away, leaving telltale oil slicks behind. Gaunt and sick from swallowing salt water, Tex Gay floated idly in his rubber boat, heedless of his badly burned leg, a shrapnel-torn left hand and bullet-punctured arm. At 6:20 a PBY patrol boat roared over the horizon. Spying the oil slicks, its pilot swooped down, waved to the figure in the lifeboat and flew on out of sight. Tex didn't mind. He knew the PBY had a patrol mission to execute. At 2:30 that afternoon, the PBY returned and he was picked up and flown to Midway for hospitalization.

Targets and Victims of a Hate Campaign

Americans needed something upon which to focus their overwhelming anger at the attack on Pearl Harbor and the subsequent excesses following Japanese victories in the Far East. They had no trouble finding it in the person of General Hideki Tojo, Premier and War Minister of Japan and an architect of its policy of conquest. The dour, bald, bespectacled Tojo had all the necessary qualifications to put him in the same boat with America's other two bogeymen, Hitler and Mussolini. He had a rasping, shrill voice; his nickname was Razor. LIFE joined a national press campaign that vilified him as the world's No. 1 bad guy.

Unfortunately, the understandable hatred for all things Japanese boiled over and badly burned the Nisei, Americans who had the bad luck to be of Japanese descent. Caught up in the often thoughtless hysteria of instant "Japophobia" that swept the country, these mostly loyal Americans (only a handful were dangerous) were uprooted from their homes and herded into internment camps. As the war went on, the hysteria calmed down, thanks in no small part to the heroism of Nisei battalions that fought with Allied armies in Europe. Even so, their interned relatives were held in remote places of confinement until a few months before the war's end.

Japanese-Americans, carrying the few belongings they were allowed to take with them, trudge through the dust past hastily built dormitories in a California internment camp called Manzanar, where they spent the next three years. LIFE said the vanguard of recently displaced Nisei were "settled comfortably" in their new home and were "prepared to wait out the war in willing and not unprofitable internment."

Two weeks after the attack on Pearl Harbor, LIFE ran this Baltimore *Sun* cartoon of a leering Japan plunging a burning stake into the Pacific.

earthy yellow complexion

less frequent epicanthic fold

flatter nose

sometimes rosy cheeks

heavy beard

broader, shorter face

massive cheek and jawbone

parchment yellow complexion

more frequent epicanthic fold

higher bridge

never has rosy cheeks

lighter facial bones

longer, narrower face

scant beard

Faces scored like anatomical charts, a grim Tojo and a smiling Chinese were part of a LIFE article called "How to Tell Japs from the Chinese."

Wearing a chestful of military medals and carrying a long-bladed samurai sword, Tojo "stands at respectful attention only before his emperor."

American artists fire a barrage exhorting everyone to

This is the Enemy

THIS IS THE ENEMY

Published by LIFE one year after Pearl Harbor, these posters (which appeared in a show at New York's Museum of Modern Art) are among the 2,224 such works by artists "armed with paintbrushes, canvas, paper and terrific determination to arouse the nation to winning the fight." If their purpose as posters was to portray the enemy as brutal hangmen, slave drivers and mass murderers, they succeeded. Leering, bestial yellow men were shown menacing white women—a favorite subject of propagandists. Other posters urged citizens to stock up on War Bonds, while others, in colorful tableaux, recommended variations on the theme: "Zip your lip or sink a ship."

FOR Victory
BUY MORE WAR BONDS · STAMPS

SLAVE WORLD - OR FREE WORLD?

GO WITHOUT
SO THEY WON'T HAVE TO

Buna: the Road Back

America's counteroffensive in the Far East began with overlapping campaigns—in the Solomon Islands and, approximately 500 miles west, on the Papuan peninsula of New Guinea. By January 1943, the Japanese—who had invaded the island of New Guinea at Buna months before and had threatened Australian and U.S. forces under Douglas MacArthur at Port Moresby—were forced back to Buna Mission. The battle that followed was photographed by LIFE photographer George Strock. It was often a nightmare of hand-to-hand combat in jungle so thick that "in the dark, live Americans bumped into live Japs," while daylight would reveal "dead Americans . . . alongside dead Japs."

After six weeks of desperate fighting, an impatient MacArthur rushed in fresh troops under Lieutenant General Robert Eichelberger, whose orders were: "Take Buna or don't come back alive." Eichelberger did take Buna—but the operation required another month and cost 787 American lives.

After the battle, Buna's jungle is desolate shambles of blasted tree and countless shell holes filled wit water from tropical rains.

◀An Australian infantryman blinded at Buna by an exploding shell i helped to the rear by a Papuan ab origine in George Silk's historic pic ture. "Scarcely more than a genera tion ago," commented LIFE, "the tribesmen were head-hunters."

German-born Herman Bottcher, standout combatant in the Papuan campaign, led American troops on drive that split Japanese defenses "All he wants," said LIFE, "is fu U.S. citizenship."

Gaunt and unshaven, a reconnaissance patrol armed with rifles and submachine guns poses for George Strock after completing a mission.

General Eichelberger, one-time Superintendent at West Point, pauses for tea. He gained the confidence of GIs by slogging into battle with them.

A GI stands over a Japanese soldier he shot with a .45 pistol. The dying man and his comrades were sniping from the landing barge at left when they were killed. "The Americans would have preferred to take them prisoners," said LIFE, "but the Japs were not willing." "Words are never enough," commented LIFE when it printed this photograph of three Americans cut down on Buna beach near a wrecked landing craft. Released after the War Department lifted censorship on combat casualties, this picture by George Strock shocked Americans at home. ▶

1942-1943

Guadalcanal Saga

Guadalcanal pilot

On a timetable roughly matching the MacArthur forces' strike northward from the Australian subcontinent, the U.S. command began executing plans to roll back the Japanese offensive from its easternmost Pacific reaches in the Solomon Islands. The invasion of Guadalcanal by U.S. Marines was the opening round in a vast, three-year campaign of island-hopping. "Guadal" caught the imagination of Americans eager for news of counterattack, and was followed anxiously in the press. Among LIFE's teams were John Hersey, who wrote of Marine heroism, and Ralph Morse, who photographed it

along with the naval action off Guadalcanal. Morse lost his film on that assignment, but returned re-equipped to the island when the Army took over for the exhausted Marines.

The Guadalcanal story was one of mosquitoes, snakes, dysentery, drenching jungles and an unorthodox enemy who sniped from trees and rampaged at night in suicidal "banzai" attacks. But when the Japanese retired after six months, they left behind them 24,000 dead. U.S. casualties were 1,752 dead and 4,245 wounded, but thousands more, most of them in the First Marine Division, were felled by malaria.

GIs on patrol, wary of hidden Japanese, push cautiously through the jungle.

An early report on what 'Guadal' was like

John Hersey accompanied a detachment of Marines in the third (and crucial) battle of the Matanikau River on Guadalcanal. His report to LIFE, a part of it reprinted here, was later expanded in Hersey's book Into the Valley.

We had reason to hope that our job would be a pushover. Just a sniper or two to hunt down and kill. We were about 75 feet from the river when we found out how wrong our hope was. The signal was a single shot from a sniper. A couple of seconds after it, snipers all around opened up on us. Machine guns from across the river opened up. But the terrible thing was that Jap mortars over there opened up too. Beside the mortar shelling, the sniper fire and even machine gun fire, with its high, small-sounding report, seemed a mere botheration. But each mortar explosion was a visitation of death.

When the first bolts of this awful thunder began to fall among us, we hit the ground. We were like earthy insects with some great foot being set down in our midst, and we scurried for little crannies—cavities under the roots of huge trees, little gullies, dead logs. Explosions were about 10 seconds apart, and all around us, now 50 yards away, now 20 feet. And all the while snipers and machine gunners wrote in their nasty punctuation.

When fear began to be epidemic in that closed-in place, no one could resist it and soon the word came whispering back: "Withdraw . . . withdraw . . . withdraw. . . ." It was then that Marine Captain Charles Alfred Rigaud, the boy with tired circles under his eyes, showed himself a good officer and grown man. He stood up on his feet, despite the snipers, and shouted out: "Who in Christ's name gave that order?" This was enough to freeze the men in their tracks. Next, by a combination of blistering sarcasm, orders and cajolery, he not only got the men back into position, he got them in a mood to fight again. I am certain that Captain Rigaud was just as terrified as I was (i.e., plenty), for he was eminently human. And yet his rallying those men was as cool a performance as you can imagine.

Ralph Morse photographed battle-strained soldiers pausing, near a fox-hole on a Guadalcanal knoll, to clean weapons that rusted in the humidity.

LIFE's map locates the Guadalcanal airfield *(cross)*, from which pilots attacked warships and transports attempting to reinforce the island.

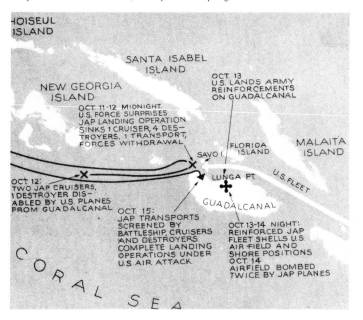

CHOISEUL ISLAND

SANTA ISABEL ISLAND

NEW GEORGIA ISLAND

OCT. 13
U.S. LANDS ARMY
REINFORCEMENTS
ON GUADALCANAL

OCT. 11-12 MIDNIGHT.
U.S. FORCE SURPRISES
JAP LANDING OPERATION
SINKS 1 CRUISER, 4 DES-
TROYERS, 1 TRANSPORT,
FORCES WITHDRAWAL

SAVO I.

FLORIDA ISLAND

MALAITA ISLAND

OCT. 12:
TWO JAP CRUISERS,
1 DESTROYER DIS-
ABLED BY U.S. PLANES
FROM GUADALCANAL

LUNGA PT.

U.S. FLEET

GUADALCANAL

OCT. 15:
JAP TRANSPORTS
SCREENED BY
BATTLESHIP, CRUISERS
AND DESTROYERS
COMPLETE LANDING
OPERATIONS UNDER
U.S. AIR ATTACK

OCT. 13-14 NIGHT:
REINFORCED JAP
FLEET SHELLS U.S.
AIR FIELD AND
SHORE POSITIONS
OCT. 14
AIRFIELD BOMBED
TWICE BY JAP PLANES

CORAL SEA

At battle's end, soldiers with soap and pails balanced on a felled tree stand in a jungle stream and wash their grimy clothes and bodies.

133

In this dramatic painting by LIFE artist Tom Lea, a brilliant fan of orange flame shoots hundreds of feet into the air and black smoke boils skyward as bombs in the *Wasp's* forward magazine detonate. She was struck by torpedoes from a Japanese submarine. Lea, aboard an escort ship, witnessed the flattop's death off Guadalcanal on September 15, 1942. He was as stunned by the unexpected loss of the giant carrier as was the

Navy, which also lost the *Hornet*, four destroyers and two cruisers in the seesaw Guadalcanal naval battle. "I felt very depressed while painting it," Lea wrote. "The colors are poor, inadequate symbols of the real tragedy, and whether the picture shows the tragedy, I do not know. It is so strange to put a howling inferno into the middle of a soft and beautiful sky and an untroubled tropic sea. Yet that's how it was."

Al Schmid, hero, comes home from Guadalcanal

The story of Al Schmid (a Marine who was nearly blinded while killing 200 Japanese as they tried to cross Guadalcanal's Tenaru River) appeared in LIFE under senior editor Roger Butterfield's byline. Excerpted here, the story later became a movie, Pride of the Marines, starring John Garfield.

The Japs were coming over in gangs of 35 to 50 and Al was cutting them down in batches. A bullet caught Lee, his loader, in the arm. He couldn't load any more, but he could still help. Al was loading and firing both; when he'd get close to the end of a belt, Lee would punch his arm, and he would fire a quick burst, rip open the magazine and insert a new belt.

Of the 1,200 Japs who tried to cross the Tenaru River that night, 18 were wounded, two were captured and the rest killed. But somewhere one managed to get through, for suddenly there was a blinding flash and explosion and something hit Al a terrific wallop in the face. It was a hand grenade and when Al put his hand up all he could feel was a wet, sticky pulp. Lee heard him fussing with his .45 and yelled, "Don't do it, Smitty, don't shoot yourself!" "Hell," said Al, "don't worry about that. I'm going to get the first Jap that comes in here." "But you can't see him," Lee told him. "Just tell me which way he's coming from and I'll get him," said Al. Hours later, Al was carried back to a dressing station. He heard the lieutenant's voice and held out the .45. "I guess I won't need this any more, sir," he said. Then he passed out.

Almost blind, Al Schmid relaxes with his fiancée, Ruth Hartley, on a Philadelphia porch.

Killed as they charged machine guns manned by Al Schmid and fellow Marines, Japanese soldiers lie in the mud of the Tenaru River.

The charred head of a Japanese tankman is displayed on a tank following a fierce battle on a Guadalcanal beach. LIFE photographer

Ralph Morse snapped the gory picture after U.S. troops removed the head from the knocked-out tank. Such scenes were not unusual on

Guadalcanal, where the stench of corpses filled the air, and the remains of Japanese defenders quickly decomposed in the heat.

Waiting for a soldier

Watching for an airman

Wives, Mothers and Sweethearts

The women war left behind—and there were millions of them in the United States—were as active as their menfolk abroad, and some were very busy indeed, clocking long hours in defense plants and in uniform (*overleaf*). For such women, good pay could mean good living. But those who remained at home with children found it difficult to subsist without their husbands' peacetime earnings. Some clubbed together in an ingenious expedient called "tripling up." To make ends meet, they shared the rent, split weekly food bills and rotated housekeeping chores—an arrangement that left over enough to enable the group members to buy War Bonds. Women also played their part by keeping homes intact and staying in touch with their absent men—a role, LIFE noted, that "is not the least part of the battle."

Three service wives from Queens, New York, survive the war with their children in a shared apartment. Combined income: $380 a month.

A Phoenix, Arizona, war worker pens her Navy boyfriend a thank-you note for sending her a souvenir—a Japanese skull he found on New Guinea.

In Mishawaka, Indiana, a proud Mabel Smith walks with her sons home on furlough. "Womanlike," offered LIFE, "she is out of step."

Mishawaka mother Smith was LIFE's model war mom, who "to her boys stands for home, love, faith, all the things they are fighting for."

In her kitchen Mrs. Smith whips batter while preparing her furloughed boys' favorite dessert—devil's food cake with chocolate frosting.

Women at War

World War II may have been the most important single liberating influence in the recent history of women, but at the time, it seemed that everybody was just doing what had to be done. Johnny, if he was not 4-F, signed up as a soldier; and Jane took his place or joined the service herself, another almost unprecedented U.S. military experience. LIFE covered the whole phenomenon of women participating in the war in stories on the WAACs, the WAVEs, and the women Marines—as well as on that legendary industrial figure, Rosie the Riveter.

Despite her sexist sobriquet, Rosie was enormously important. In the aviation industry alone, the proportion of women employees zoomed from 1 per cent in 1941 to an astonishing 65 per cent in 1943. And in most heavy industries, from which men had traditionally barred them, women discovered in the sudden urgency of wartime production what they had suspected all along—that there was nothing in their makeup that made them incapable of performing as well as their male counterparts and often better.

Schoolgirl volunteer

Army officer-nurse

U.S. Navy cover girl

LIFE sent Margaret Bourke-White to Gary, Indiana, where she found women like this one working at the lip of an open-hearth steel furnace.

Indiana torch-bearer   Housewife-nurses' aide   Oklahoma WAVE trainees   Junior nurse's capping   Air Force ferry pilot

A windblown ferry pilot solos her trainer plane over a field in Texas. She was a member of the Women's Flying Training Detachment.

◄ These WAACs have just donned their first gas masks. LIFE said they promptly burst into giggles, sounding like "a flock of muffled pigeons."

Ready for take-off, pilot-in-training Nancy Nesbit of Pomona, California, checks with the Avenger Field control tower for instructions.

'Rosie the Riveter' takes over the toughest jobs

Women workers were often handier than men in assembling airplane parts at Consolidated Aircraft's new plant in Fort Worth, Texas.

Movie star Veronica Lake demonstrates the dangers of wearing her peek-a-boo hairdo at a drill press. ▼ She later put hers up in braids.

An engineering trainee employed by Curtiss-Wright adjusts a wind-direction indicator placed on top of a classroom building.

A bandannaed member of a female section gang works on maintenance of a length of Northern Pacific Railway track in Washington State.

A meat-packing plant worker hoses ▶ down a side of beef. Women also toiled as garbage collectors, truck and bus drivers, crane operators, sign painters, plumbers and stevedores on the waterfront.

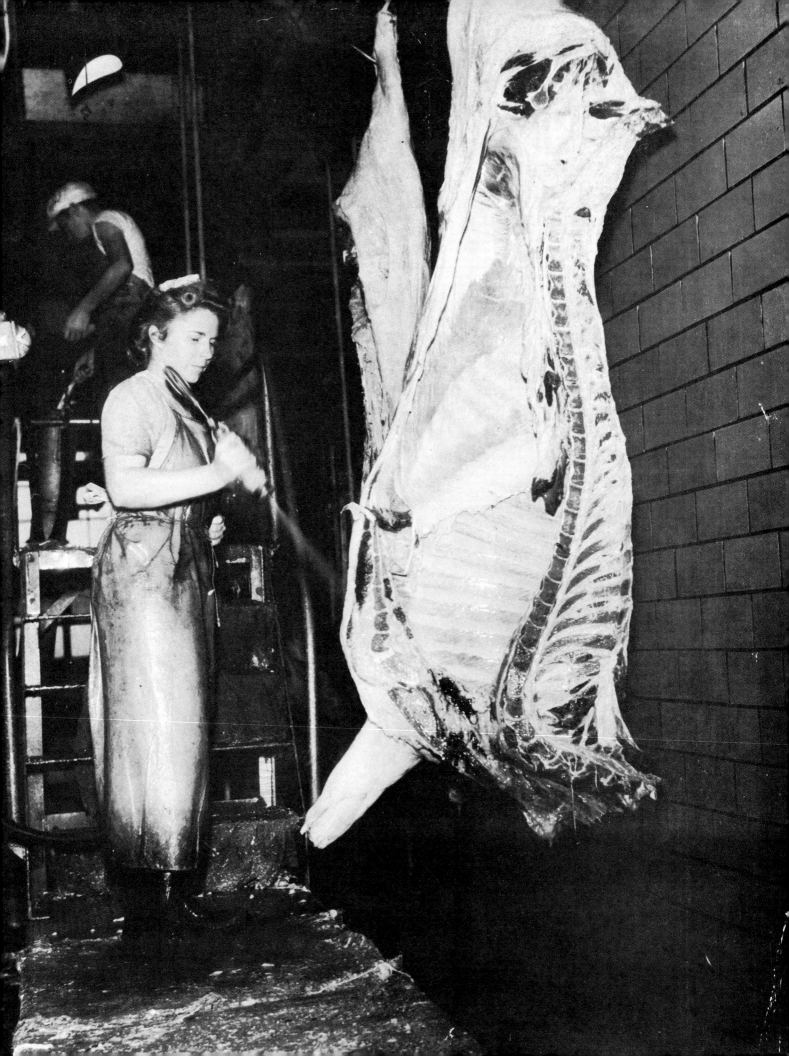

Blacks in Uniform: a Proud Tradition

Almost alone among major U.S. publications, LIFE during World War II championed the cause of blacks in combat. It did so at a time when many white Americans (including most of the service chiefs and members of Congress) felt blacks should be limited to traditional military roles of mess boy, cook, steward, messenger and truck driver.

LIFE's concern was partly moral, but mostly patriotic; the magazine's editors wanted to see black manpower put where it would "do the most good." Thus it ran several articles on black combat soldiers in training, including one in 1942 that traced the history of black troops from the Boston Massacre of 1770

to World War I, when a black regiment "never gave a foot of ground, never lost a prisoner, was the first Allied regiment to reach the Rhine." It described, in World War II, black engineers at work on roads in Burma, and the famous "Red Ball Express" that ran from Normandy to the German front.

What LIFE could not gloss over was the fact that the military was almost totally segregated. "It is perfectly true that U.S. Negroes have never had a square deal from the U.S. white majority," it said. "But they know their lot would be far worse under the racial fanatics of the Axis. Now they are glad to work and fight and die alongside their white fellow-citizens."

Using walkie-talkies, a black lieutenant and a white major direct live ammunition training. Officers could mingle; enlisted men could not.

Family and friends of a GI named Raymond Carlton, fresh from basic training at Fort Bragg, North Carolina, admire the recruit's uniform. ▼

◀A tank manned by three noncoms and a technician-gunner attached to the all-black 758th Tank Battalion maneuvers in Louisiana.

▲During artillery practice at Fort Huachuca, Arizona, enlisted men line up a target for their guns with a tripod-mounted aiming circle.

British Tommies leave their base at Tobruk and advance across the Libyan desert toward German lines as a shell

1942-1943

Desert hero Montgomery

Monty and the Fox

By 1942 the North African desert war had escalated from a cockpit conflict into a major theater. German Afrika Korps troops had reinforced the Italians that faced small British forces, and the Allies realized they badly needed a desert victory before they could attack the Axis' Fortress Europe. This crucial battle pitted two of the war's most flamboyant generals against each other. In the Allied camp was Lieutenant General Bernard Law Montgomery, a by-the-book perfectionist who sported a rakish beret and chafed at taking orders. German-Italian forces were led by Erwin Rommel, a tank genius who rode into combat like an old-fashioned cavalry commander, and was so adept at surprising and bloodying Allied armor that he was dubbed the Desert Fox.

Montgomery finally stopped the Fox at his deepest penetration into Allied territory—an Egyptian railway station just 65 miles from Alexandria called El Alamein. Then, covered by a thousand-gun barrage, 1,114 tanks smashed the weary Afrika Korps. With Montgomery in pursuit, Rommel retreated across North Africa, stopping finally in Tunisia, where he hoped to regroup and fight another day.

British tanks, nicknamed Waltzing Matildas, lumber across the Libyan desert. The 25-ton Matildas were the battleships of the British tank arse-nal. But they were slower than the panzers and, while well armored, carried a 40mm gun easily outranged by the German 75mm.

The tanks talk back and forth in a dusty desert battle

The eminent British author Alan Moorehead was a war correspondent who served in Africa with Montgomery's Eighth Army, among many other theaters. From the second—and decisive—battle of El Alamein he cabled LIFE an account of what a tank battle is all about, from which the following excerpt is taken:

Unless you are in a tank yourself, you don't see anything very clearly in a tank battle. The enemy appears as just a line of tiny silhouettes where the sky hits the desert, dark silhouettes shaped exactly like distant battleships, each one spitting out a yellow flash from time to time. Your own tanks, weaving in to attack, disappear behind the wake of their own dust. Within a few minutes it is just so much smoke, dust, flame and noise.

"There they come," yells someone on his radio blower. Listening on a headquarters communication vehicle, you hear the tanks talking to one another right in the battle. You hear: "Get to hell out of it Bill so that I can get at this - - - -. Easy boy, easy boy, now at him. . . . Bill, you - - - -, you're blocking my way again. . . . Look out, right

fired by defending German artillery explodes behind them (the puff of smoke on the ridge at the center).

Dressed for the desert in a greatcoat and protective goggles, Rommel played the fox to the Allies' hounds across most of North Africa.

◄ Italian soldiers surrender to a British soldier. Such mass defections hurt Rommel, who was usually short of troops as well as supplies.

behind you." And through it all you hear the bursting of shells, the tearing and screaming of the tank treads, the gears grunting into reverse and forward. No one, remember, who wasn't right in this first fight had any clear idea of what was going on. We had to wait and just watch that pall of battle smoke widen, darken and move west.

Then a staff major came out of it and told us: "They came right at us off the rising ground with the sun behind their backs. Right smack at us. They opened up with their 50mm gun at 1,500 yards—much too far for our 37s. So the boys just went into the barrage hull down at 40 mph to get into range. Then they mixed it. I tell you no one on God's earth can follow what's going on. The boys are just weaving in and out between the Jerries, passing right through them, then turning and coming back into it again. They're passing 50 and 60 yards apart and firing at point-blank range. As soon as you see a Swastika you just let fly. There's everything in the air—tracers, shells, bullets, ricochets, incendiaries and bits of red-hot metal whanging off the burning tanks. Some of the tanks are blowing right up into the air, their petrol exploding, their ammunition popping off in every direction."

Every few minutes a tank would stay out of the battle, rush to a supply vehicle, fling in petrol and shells, then zigzag into the arena again. The battle died down little by little as dusk fell, a blue-green dusk lightened in the east by the red glare of burning tanks.

A German Mark IV tank and its crew wait out a sandstorm. The 22-ton tank was the star of Rommel's Afrika Korps. It was faster and more ma- neuverable than most Allied tanks and was fitted with an extra-large fuel tank that enabled it to travel 125 miles without refueling.

A soldier's Christmas

A Tunisian burial

U.S. Baptism of Fire in North Africa

In November 1942 Americans from Scotland and the U.S. landed on hostile soil across the Atlantic for the first time. They found the going much to their liking at the outset. Troops under a comparatively unknown major general named George Patton took the Moroccan towns of Port Lyautey and Safi within two days. After negotiations with Vichyite Admiral Jean Darlan, all resistance in Morocco and Algeria ceased.

But the cushy soldiering stopped abruptly when Allied forces reached Tunisia. There they clashed with Germans under the direction of a tough, brilliant field marshal named Albert Kesselring, who, operating from Italy, instantly reinforced his Tunisian troops to battle the Allies to a three-month standstill. In their first important fight, at Kasserine Pass in the Tebessa Mountains of Tunisia, the untried GIs took a shellacking, and 2,400 men surrendered after 192 had been killed. The news of this reverse naturally generated elation in Germany. The "big-mouthed Yankees," chortled Nazi propaganda chief Goebbels, had not even met select German soldiers. On the American side, the setback shocked the high command, which relieved some generals and turned the best ones—like Patton—loose to stiffen discipline and drive their newly blooded veterans across Tunisia to link up eventually with the British Eighth Army and finish off the Germans in Africa.

LIFE artist Fletcher Martin's conception of the desperate fire fight on Tunisia's Hill 609, which occurred after an obscuring cloud had abruptly lifted and the Americans *(right)* saw the Germans *(left)* only 15 yards away. The sudden battle ended after some 40 Germans were killed.

In this Eliot Elisofon photograph, GIs charge toward a Tunisian oasis called Sened. Top officers concerned about their troops' performance asked to see Elisofon's pictures; comments ranged from gripes about unmanned machine guns to praise for textbook-perfect deployment.

Germany's adventure in the desert ends at Tunis

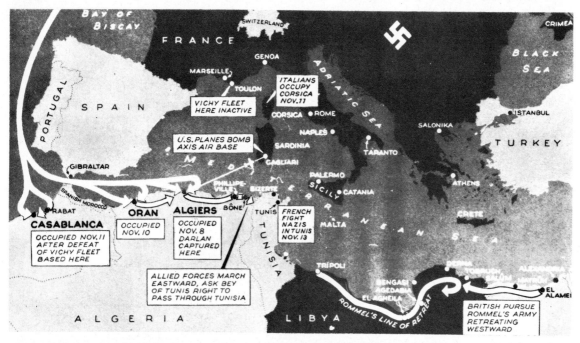

The collapse of Axis forces in North Africa is summed up in this map, which LIFE ran in November 1942. By this time, the Americans had occupied Casablanca and stormed the Vichy French strongholds of Oran and Algiers from the west, while Montgomery's Eighth Army pursued Rommel's Afrika Korps across the Libyan desert.

American infantrymen in Tunisia take refuge, during a German dive-bomber attack, in foxholes dug into the underside of an embankment.

Buoyed by the success of the North African landings, F.D.R. and Churchill meet in Casablanca to plan for the Axis' "unconditional surrender."

GIs toss German helmets into a pile—a scene that more than any other in the bloody African war signified the defeat of Rommel's army. ▼

"This Hitler superman is now a prisoner in Tunisia," said LIFE of an unshaven, Afrika Korpsman who, unlike his fanatical Japanese Axis-partners, surrendered when beaten. During the Tunisian campaign, almost 300,000 German and Italian troops followed his example.

151

1942-1943

LIFE

APRIL 5, 1943   10 CENTS

Monty's beret

Shortages and Chic

Neither Paris nor Seventh Avenue, but the U.S. War Production Board was the arbiter of fashion for much of America in the early 1940s; rigid sumptuary regulations limited use of scarce materials, hem depth and skirt width. The WPB decree: no cuffs, no ruffles, no flap pockets and the legs of the newly popular pants could be no more than 19 inches wide. Out went baubles, bangles and beads; in came austerity and the soberly utilitarian, as shortages of silk, rayon and the new miracle fiber, nylon—ideal for parachutes—cut into frivolity.

American women weren't fazed in the slightest. They found that military hats—GIs' or generals'—men's pants, or a strategically placed patch could create instant chic. LIFE's fashion department had a field day.

Nancy Guild modeled a GI fatigue hat as a University of Arizona freshman and a week after LIFE's picture appeared won a Hollywood contract.

LIFE

APRIL 20, 1942   10 CENTS

Woman in pants

LIFE found patches of sunshine in the sartorial gloom: this young woman decorated a picture-story on how to mend worn clothing.

Addressing the problems created by stocking shortages, LIFE compared alternatives in this photograph: "S" stood for rayon stockings, "P" for stocking-colored paint, "B" for bare. ▶ The article also showed readers how to apply the briefly popular paint, including the painting of seams.

Cotton stockings printed in pink and blue were the hose manufacturers' response to the challenge of rayon restrictions and short supplies of silk.

For the first time in fashion annals, women wore the pants on streets, at school and in the office. These were a bit wider than WPB regulations.

Short haircuts, considered much safer at work than long glamor bobs and less trouble, became the style—and women's army regulation.

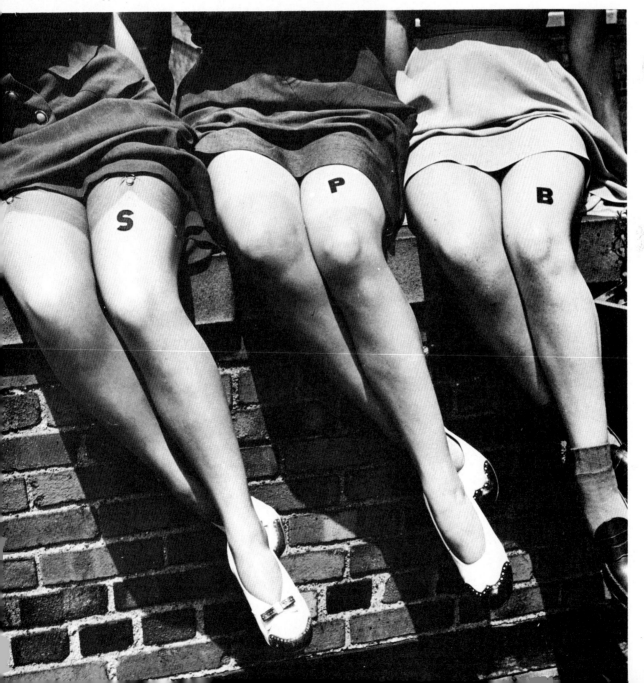

153

How to Grow a Victory Garden: The female student body of Portland, Oregon's Jane Addams High hoes a freshly plowed, 200-by-40-foot plot, recently the school's lawn. The produce the girls grew was put to good use in the school cafeteria, nursery school and home economics classes.

Rush to Resourcefulness: Do-It-Yourself

When food and gas and skilled hands ran short at home, people revived the traditional American ideal of making do and transformed it into the modern concept of do-it-yourself. Americans who had thought themselves incapable of changing a light bulb necessarily became apt, if not expert, handymen. And city folk who had never cultivated more than a window-box geranium discovered that they could grow their own food in impromptu gardens.

Encouraging the trend, LIFE published "how-to" features on everything from buying a horse to needlework. Knitting was a favorite subject; even before Pearl Harbor, LIFE ran a complete knitting manual and featured a pretty knitter on its cover *(page 106)*. A feature called "How to Heat Your House," in the issue dated November 2, 1942, would give a reader of the energy-critical 1970s a sharp sense of déjà vu. Referring to the fuel rationing regulations that limited house temperatures during winter, the article concluded: "The most obvious economy is implicit in the fact that U.S. homes are notoriously overheated, as rationed-oil burners will testify when they find themselves comfortable at 65°."

How to Fix a Broken Window: Practical hints for home repair, addressed to suburbanites and city dwellers whose handymen had gone to war or taken better-paying defense work, included a demonstration of replacing a pane of glass. Here is the first step—removal of the old pane.

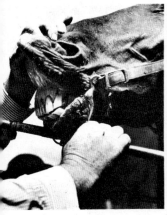 

How to Buy a Horse: Deadly serious about keeping its car-bereft readers on the road, LIFE ran instructions on purchasing alternate means of transportation. These pictures show how to determine age by looking a trading prospect in the mouth. (The horse on the left with longer teeth is older.)

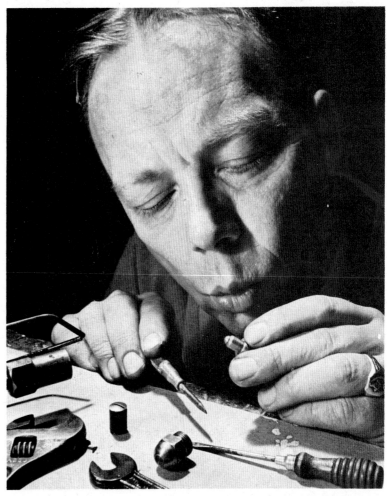

How to Store a Car: The final step in putting up the useless car was covering it, from bumper to bumper, with old newspapers.

How to Fix the Oil Burner: For delicate jobs like this—maintaining a burner's feeder nozzle—LIFE cautioned, "Clean, but do not tinker."

The Patriotic Pitch

To the Axis, wartime advertising had a hundred ways of saying "Cut your throat!" To its clients' customers at home, however, the Madison Avenue boys were careful and ingenious in finding ways to avoid saying "Eat your heart out" while the hostilities continued. Their message was that sacrifice was in order ("Lucky Strike Green Has Gone to War"), but victory would redeem all temporary deprivations. Companies whose peacetime products were no longer available to the consumer—makers of tires and phonographs, electric irons and automobiles, rubber and telephones—pointed with pride to their involvement in the war effort. They reminded their customers that all those things would be coming back when peace returned.

Bread, shirts, shoes, silver—every imaginable product—got into the patriotic act. Even furniture manufacturers became warlike, quick to note that a substantial part of their plant space was devoted to the production of war materiel. On a more dramatic note, the Pontiac Division of General Motors displayed an ad pocked with blacked-out "censored" bars, demonstrating the amount of top-secret goods they were producing for the armed forces. Finally, products that could not conceivably be linked with the war were pitched with a martial theme. It was a duty to keep fit—by brushing teeth with a favorite brand name or by just general good grooming.

The campaign was probably effective propaganda; it was certainly good P.R. for the agencies' clients when patriotism was the best product in anybody's inventory.

"IT WASN'T JUST DARK....IT WAS BLACK AS TOJO'S HEART!"...

Then suddenly our searchlights swept across ten miles of midnight...and
pinned that Jap cruiser in a blinding glare of light...we could see those Japs plain
as day, scurrying around like rats in a trap!"...

Now, the light that caught those Japs came partly from the inside of a
Chrysler engine...Sounds funny, doesn't it?...But the Superfinish process that
gave Chrysler engine parts the smoothest surface in the world is today polishing metal
reflectors for searchlights...polishing them to a mirror-like smoothness that can
send a sharp beam of light up to twenty-five miles without distortion.

Climax in the Battle of the Atlantic

Arctic convoy mariner

Troop-carrying liners

While the Allies mounted successful counterattacks in Russia, the Pacific and Africa in 1942, their predicament in the Atlantic—that water bridge across which moved precious supplies to England and Arctic Russia—was desperate. German U-boats traveling in packs were sinking ships as fast as they could fire torpedoes. In the first six months of 1942, the Allied merchant marine lost three million tons of shipping; U.S. losses in that period surpassed those of World War I.

Favorite hunting grounds for the U-boats were the busy shipping lanes around the East Coast of the United States, where in one month an appalling 28 vessels were sunk. Americans now had a new pastime: watching their own ships burning offshore.

Allied scientists as well as military strategists responded to the threat by developing antisubmarine devices: sonar, an echo-locating mechanism that enabled destroyers equipped with depth charges to detect and then strike submerged U-boats; and the new radio detection device, radar, that spotted submarines on the surface, where they were sitting ducks. Long-range aircraft were deployed to cover convoys for nearly a thousand miles from their ports, and fast escort carriers with lethal torpedo-armed aircraft shepherded ships on the remainder of their journey. Slowly the Allies turned the tables on the U-boats, and the subs became the hunted.

LIFE's artist aboard the *Campbell*

German-born Anton Otto Fischer, a U.S. Coast Guard Lieutenant Commander, painted the cruise of the cutter Campbell *for LIFE, and reported on the action at right.*

There it was on the surface, our sixth submarine in 18 hours. She was crossing our bow from port to starboard a few hundred yards ahead and couldn't have seen us in the dark. We turned to starboard to ram her but as we bore down someone on the conning tower must have seen us and she turned on a course almost parallel to ours. In a few seconds we were on top of the submarine. It was an eerie sensation. A man could have dropped from the cutter's deck to hers. As we passed in that quiet second, the sub's port hydroplane ripped through our hull. Then, as she drifted astern, all hell broke loose. Our after guns opened up, their crews hollering like a bunch of Comanche Indians. Three-inch shells were slamming into the U-boat's hull at point-blank range. You just couldn't miss. And you could see the lines of our 20mm tracers sweeping the decks, knocking men off like tenpins. Through the darkness I could hear men calling in the water, one man shouting, "Hello, boys," obviously the only two English words he knew. Then the calls grew fainter and finally died away.

From a destroyer escort, one of whose protective guns is visible at right, photographer Frank Scherschel took this picture of a convoy on a tranquil Atlantic. The following week, LIFE ran more Scherschel photographs *(overleaf)* that showed a more dangerous side of convoy duty.

In Fischer's painting, the *Campbell*, on convoy duty, bears down on a German sub and shells her before ▼ ramming her—and in turn being badly damaged. The *Campbell* is flooding and soon her searchlight will fade. She was towed 800 miles to safety. The U-boat sank.

The Murmansk Convoy to Russia via the Arctic was the roughest duty of all, cursed not only by U-boats and aerial raiders, but also by the bitter cold. Frank Scherschel made the trip for LIFE and almost didn't come back. From the top in the sequence above, he first photographed a Nazi bomber (over the stern of the tanker in the foreground) just before dropping its two torpedoes. In the second photograph, another bomber turns sharply to avoid fire. In the next picture, two more German planes (flat smudges at left) veer off after dropping torpedoes. In the next picture, an attacker is hit and plunges toward the water. The stricken pilot had machine-gunned Scherschel's ship as he passed. After he had clicked his camera once, somebody yelled, "Duck!" Scherschel did as he was told, and survived to take the picture directly above.

An Allied tanker goes up in smoke ▶ after being torpedoed by a submarine just a few miles off the Florida coast. Proximity to the U.S. offered scant protection to convoys, especially at night, since submariners used lights of cities like Miami and New York to silhouette their targets.

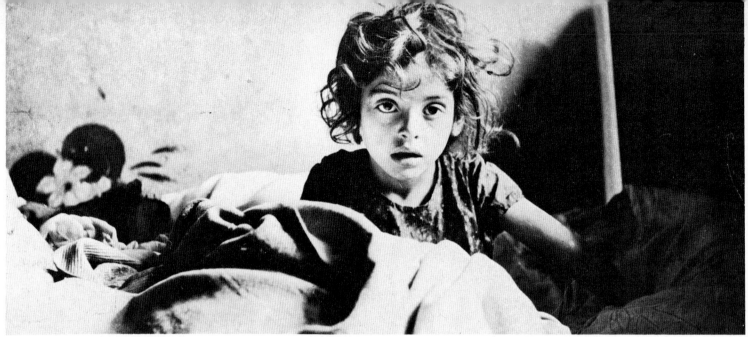

Hunger glistens in the eyes of a Polish girl who lives in bed to save strength. Other hungry children lacked strength even to forage.

A Harsh Life in Occupied Europe

"One of our greatest mistakes in the First World War," stated German Field Marshal Gerd von Rundstedt, "was to spare the lives of civilians in enemy countries. We shall be compelled to destroy at least one third of the population of all adjacent territories. We can best achieve this through systematic malnutrition—in the end far superior to machine guns. Starvation works more effectively, especially among the young." This utterance by the commander of the Wehrmacht's western front appeared in LIFE as a commentary on Adolf Hitler's policies of conquest. For some Germans, the food-

stuffs seized to implement these policies meant momentary plenty, as they feasted on Polish hams, French champagne and Dutch chocolates. For the conquered, Nazi methods meant clothing shortages, hunger and sometimes death.

Pictures smuggled out of the occupied territories—illustrating the fate of the little girl above or showing piles of corpses in Greece or Poland—testified to the results. Occasionally, as on the opposite page, privation had its light moments. But almost everywhere it brought evils that, LIFE said, would be "passed on to the next generation."

A nap at midday is taken by a dispirited Frenchman "who has nothing to do and for whom nothing is solved, who sits and waits day after day."

French citizens, already limited by the Germans to one-half pound of meat per week, queue up for their dole of four cigarettes a day.

To protest rationing that allowed one ▶ suit a year, a young Dutchman strolls an Amsterdam street, naked except for hat, shoes, socks and umbrella.

End of the Line in Russia

Stalin in triumph

By the winter of 1942, Germany's war against the Bolsheviks, begun so auspiciously in 1941, was winding down to its grim denouement. All along a 2,000-mile front that became next to impossible to supply, German armies were reeling from blows delivered by massed infantry and armor, even cavalry.

But it was at Stalingrad—the city on the Volga River that bore the name of Hitler's most hated enemy—that the Russians truly surprised the world. There, on November 19, after an incredible two-month siege in which the two sides sometimes fought for days over a few square feet of territory, fresh troops cunningly held in reserve by Stalin attacked and trapped an entire army under Field Marshal Friedrich Paulus. Paulus' cause had been lost ever since Hitler had insisted he hold the exposed city, and screamed, "I won't leave the Volga!" But Paulus did leave the Volga in February of 1943— in captivity with 23 generals and 91,000 starved, half-frozen men. The incredible Red Army then began what became, with only minor interruptions, its two-year roll-back of the Wehrmacht to the heart of Germany.

Germans ignore women fighting fires in a Caucasian town near their farthest advance.

Red cavalrymen charge across the steppes, sabers drawn. Some 50 divisions of cavalry effectively fought the Germans. They were able to concentrate much faster than their foe, pounce and then melt into the thick Russian forests, where armor was unable to follow.

A Red Army soldier, bundled against the cold in a camouflaged parka and a fur hat, guards a shattered freight ▼ train next to German corpses that have been partially stripped by scavengers. A timely retreat before Stalingrad might have saved such Germans their lives.

Dreams of conquest abort in the

As a comrade provides covering fire, a Soviet soldier armed with a submachine gun charges a group of shattered Stalingrad buildings.

A spread-eagled Soviet machine gunner rakes the enemy while another soldier begins a cautious advance toward a German post. ▼

Fateful meeting on Soviet soil

In August 1941, Hitler and Mussolini met for the 12th time, this time on the Russian front before the disastrous outcome of the German adventure at Stalingrad. From the start, Il Duce seemed ill at ease. He studied war maps, looked at ruins the Russians had left behind and visited with his token force of Italian volunteer troops. After five "fervid" days, he remarked that the destruction had left "an uncancelable memory." Hitler apparently was unmoved by the carnage. At his urging, the dictators jointly announced "the destruction of the Bolshevist danger"—an obituary that proved to be premature.

wintry rubble of Stalingrad

▲ Beaten Germans captured by Soviet troops form a long line as they plod through snow to prison camps, from which very few returned.

The shame of defeat—and the fear of an expected grim fate at the hands of their captors—shows in the numb faces of these gaunt ex-supermen. ▼

1943

Backbone of the Army

Tail gunner

Ally in training

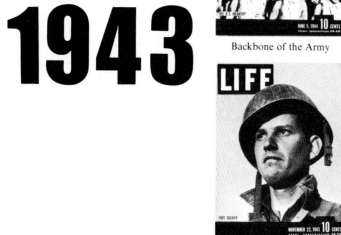

Desert veteran

Pacific vet and bride

Ike's No. 2 man

Eastern aggressor

Sky cameraman

Guerrilla "Yank" Levy

Draftee-to-be

Corn husker

Machine gunner

1944

Fredric March at "Adano"

Gift from the Pacific

U-boats' nemesis

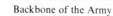

IV. COUNTERATTACK

With arms and men the Allies surge back

"With spring," said LIFE in April of 1943, "came the military offensives. And with the offensives came initial Allied successes. They were not yet big. They were not decisive. But they were guarantees that this year the Allies are determined to stay on the offensive."

By winter the forecast had been verified on all fronts. The Japanese were distancing themselves from Germany and changing their tune about bringing America to its knees. In a rare glimpse inside wartime Japan that was brought to LIFE by Claude A. Buss, a repatriated U.S. diplomat interned at Manila, the Imperial high command was seen to be preparing the Japanese for Germany's defeat, discarding the Nazis' racial theories and criticizing their conduct of the Russian war. Further, said the diplomat, the Japanese admitted that American "flappers" had capably replaced male war workers and that the U.S. Navy was winning battles.

Colossal American production and the Allies' rapid education in the techniques of total war were indeed beginning to tell. Air power, strategic and tactical, was coming of age. Germany's factories, cities and supply lines were being pounded by bombers as her forces in the field were being strafed and bombed. And in the Pacific, amphibious assaults were being made on strategic islands for the northward leap-frogging that would provide air bases for a similar pasting of Japan.

But it still took the infantry to secure territory. To get the foot soldiers onto enemy-held soil, Admiral Chester Nimitz and General Douglas MacArthur launched the amphibious operation called Cartwheel at the same time as British and American armies prepared to invade Italy by way of Sicily. General Dwight D. Eisenhower was recalled to England to prepare for the big continental invasion to come, Overlord. Cartwheel was designed to take over Japan's great Rabaul base, free MacArthur to attack the Philippines and start Nimitz off on his spectacular Central Pacific campaign. Cartwheel's western phase, up New Britain through jungles infested with leeches, fire ants, giant mosquitoes, fungus and Japanese snipers, was won by fire power and sheer guts. The eastern, island-hopping phase—Tarawa, Makin, Kwajalein, Eniwetok—progressed with ever more frightful death

tolls that demonstrated the high price of coral, as Marine Captain George P. Hunt (later LIFE's managing editor) put it. In the mountainous jungles of the long-ignored China-Burma-India theater, frustration slowly turned to heroic comeback. In the equally forlorn Aleutians, Attu was taken in a nightmare of fog and fire.

The Italian campaign was calculated to put Allied air forces within striking distance of additional industrial targets and to keep German forces pinned down. Italy did not live up to its advance billing—"the soft underbelly of Europe." Mountains and a comparatively few stubborn, skillful and well-entrenched Germans made every inch of real estate dear. It was the Allies who were pinned down—until the end of the war.

As the time for breaching Hitler's west wall approached, Allied bombers slowly gained the ascendency. When Ike briefed his invasion forces on D-minus-one, he would be able to say, "If you see an aircraft overhead, you can be virtually certain that it is one of ours."

LIFE lauded the war workers (even "boy power" was now being used); urged readers to salvage waste paper and collect "Junk for Wampum" to be sent to Pacific-based GIs to trade, presumably for coconuts; photographed sailors rowing with their girls in Central Park; and memorialized the Lindy Hop in a 10-page essay. Frank Sinatra—the earliest draftees had been certain he could never rival Bing Crosby—sang with the New York Philharmonic. Meanwhile, "Eunice from Tunis," a laundered version of the GIs' "Dirty Gertie from Bizerte" was a 90-minute wonder. The magazine paid homage to the returned heroes, and dreamed up ways of honoring those still in the thick of the action. For a Kentuckian, Sergeant Thomas Grant of the First Armored Division in Africa, it showed pictures of the six-month-old daughter he had never seen, and wrote him an open letter expressing the hope that "you will be able to see her for yourself before long."

Even as the U.S. Army's all-volunteer 442nd Regiment of second-generation Japanese-Americans was quietly setting records for valor citations in Italy, photographer Carl Mydans did a humane essay on the Japanese-Americans locked in a camp by the U.S. at Tule Lake Segregation Center in Newell, California. In *So Proudly We Hail*, Hollywood reproduced Mel Jacoby's pictures of Bataan, and everybody cried when Spencer Tracy played a ghost in *A Guy Named Joe*. A portentous development indicative of U.S. productive might almost went unnoticed. The jeep was released for civilian use down on the farm. And as the Yanks sang "Monday I Kissed Her on the Ankle" in Piccadilly, D-Day was just around the corner.

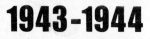

Island fighting

Opening Gun in a Mighty Offensive

On the night of December 14, 1943, a fleet of American LSTs (initials standing for Landing Ship, Tank) crept across the Coral Sea toward the jungle on the southern coast of Japanese-held New Britain. This was the first island invasion of Operation Cartwheel, a sea-spanning, pincer-like operation that was aimed at the great Japanese naval base of Rabaul, on New Britain's eastern tip. Rabaul was the apex of an immense, squat triangle, based on New Guinea to the southwest and Guadalcanal to the southeast, that aimed toward Japan. The

Australians captured Japan's New Guinea supply base at Lae, with the help of General George C. Kenney's Fifth Air Force *(pages 186–187)*. Meanwhile troops under General MacArthur's command landed on New Britain and hacked their way through the jungle up the left leg of the triangle. Amphibious forces under Admiral William F. Halsey were to make their way from Guadalcanal up the islands of the eastern leg by way of New Georgia and Bougainville. The entire Cartwheel operation was coordinated with a series of leaps up

Following the landing, GIs, under threat of enemy planes, feverishly work into the night unloading supplies from the great maws of the LSTs. Barrels of fuel tumble down ramps into the water, and are then heaved up to supply dumps on the sand, as men with faint red lamps indicate where they are to go.

the Central Pacific's Gilbert and Marshall islands: Tarawa, Eniwetok, Kwajalein and points north.

Although LSTs had been used as part of the air-land-and-sea Lae battle, the New Britain attack marked their first use in the completely amphibious island-hopping campaign that was to continue all the way to the Philippines and Japan's home islands. LIFE combat artist David Fredenthal was in an early wave of the New Britain assault. Before dawn the task force off the New Britain coast split into several units. As the main force prepared to hit the beach at Arawe, a commando-trained group of 150 landed three miles down the coast to divert Japanese fire and cut off any enemy retreat. Inside the reefs and within 30 yards of the shore, they were hit with machine-gun fire and half the diversionary force was lost. But the main force survived and started what was to become a familiar sequence: hacking a clearing in the jungle; building an air base or reconstructing a Japanese one; and preparing to invade the next island once the air cover was ready.

Paratroops, and MacArthur, precede the attack on Lae

From a Flying Fortress port, General MacArthur watches the Allied landing of paratroopers who attacked on Lae with Australian land forces.

An Australian killed when his LCI was hit by a Japanese bomber lies on a stretcher awaiting burial. He was among the few fatal casualties. ▼

◄ At the height of the parachute attack north of Lae, 10 low-flying C-53 transports drop troops into New Guinea's grassy Markham valley. Some paratroopers had already landed and spilled their chutes. At far left, another contingent drops from transports obscured behind a smoke screen.

The Marines take Tarawa in the toughest battle to date

In the bloody eastern phase of Operation Cartwheel, U.S. Marines who landed on Tarawa attack from the water's edge over a coconut-log retaining wall *(top, left)*. Of some 5,000 in the assault, 1,026 died. This capture of the key to the Gilbert Islands was a victory more dearly won than Guadalcanal or the World War I Battle of Château-Thierry.

▲The attackers, exposed to fire from hidden Japanese, swarm over a blockhouse as an oil dump explodes. The only way to destroy such a blockhouse was to swarm up to the roof and fire down on its occupants.

◀With Japanese defenders on three sides, a Marine hurls a hand grenade. At right an exhausted Marine drinks water, always a precious commodity in the tropical fighting.

Marines with carbines march off a prisoner, stripped to make sure he had no hidden weapons. Few prisoners were taken on Tarawa.

175

Defenders die hard at Eniwetok and Kwajalein

A Marine from Boat 13 drags a dead comrade out of the Engebi surf

Boat 13 picks a bad beach

On February 17, 1944, a task force attacked and in six days secured the islands of the Eniwetok Atoll. With a party in Boat 13 attacking Engebi, the first of the islands, were LIFE's George Strock and Richard Wilcox. Wilcox reported the nearly disastrous consequences of their landing in front of a Japanese pillbox.

We sprinted low through the milky surf and dropped flat on the hard coral sand. The rendezvous was complete. Boat 13 had delivered her men. One of these men rose to his knees for an instant, spun and then dropped on his back; the blood welled out of his chest and soaked his jacket. Boat 13 had come ashore squarely in front of a Jap pillbox that the first assault waves had overrun and left as dead.

Now it had suddenly come back to life, with machine guns and rifles raking the shoreline at point-blank range. To move up or down that beach was to court death. The only escape was to take cover in the water, behind a hump in the beach, and crab your way to one flank or the other.

Not all of the men of Boat 13 reached the slight safety of the water. A big, white-faced farm lad stopped crawling as a bullet went through his head. Those who reached the water lay flat under the waves, only their green helmets and faces above the froth.

A yard to the right of us a man swore a round Marine oath as a bullet dropped him completely beneath the waves to be still for eternity. One of his comrades hooked a hand under his collar and laboriously dragged him across a coral head above the surface where he could at least have the last decency of the air and the sun. To the left of us another man jerked piteously halfway between sand and sea before death stilled his suffering.

The men of Boat 13 lay behind a jeep, helpless and scared, watching the Marines die about us for half an hour. None of them said much as they lay in the water. The weight of water-soaked packs, the vomiting that came from swallowing sea water, the burning coral gashes along arms and legs, the pummeling of the surf were minor strains in the gigantic pattern of animal existence. Only the enemy guns and the dead in the water were real.

But now, while some of their fellows distracted the Japs in the pillbox by shots from the surf, men from behind the jeep began to trickle ashore to the right and left of the pillbox. Once ashore they ran in swift zigzags, dropping to protect themselves from the fire of snipers, then rising to move in behind the pillbox. Their faces were set with anger and their hands made fists around the hard yellow steel of grenades. As they moved in they could see the men they had left still lying in the surf, crouched behind the jeep. Their work was short and their aim excellent. Sullen puffs of smoke spread up and out from the emplacement and a fine shower of concrete rained into the water. The men of Boat 13 proceeded with their landing on Engebi Island.

A Japanese soldier burns in his foxhole after he was hit by an American's flame thrower in the savage fighting for Engebi, one of the 38 islands of the Eniwetok Atoll. The pictures here were made by George Strock, whom many consider the war's greatest combat photographer.

After the fighting for Kwajalein, among the last of the Marshall Islands to be recaptured, a Japanese artilleryman lies dead by his gun.

1943-1944

Volunteer USO beauty

Morale Boosters

For many GIs, Saturday nights were likely to be the loneliest of a lifetime. But for some—and the number grew as the war continued—it brought a boyhood fantasy come true: bevies of beautiful women bent on pleasuring the boys. Broadway and Hollywood stars and starlets attracted the most attention among these morale boosters, but their ranks were swelled with unknowns, amateurs and home-front volunteers. Occasionally joined by male entertainers and abetted by the USO, the nongovernment servicemen's organization, they brought bright moments to troops everywhere.

The entertainments, ranging from full-scale Broadway musicals to amateur nights and dates with celebrities, were staged from Maine to New Mexico, and behind the front lines of the South Pacific and Europe. As the fantasies bloomed, the editors of LIFE, delighted with the chance to combine their two best-read stories—showbiz and war—seized the opportunity whenever they could.

LIFE followed starlet Marilyn Hare on her unusual pursuit: to kiss 10,000 soldiers. At a California Army camp, she collects a few in return.

Rita Hayworth mends a hole in Private Luther Eklund's pants. He and seven buddies came to visit Rita when she was unable to make an appearance on their California base.

◄ A young Dorothy McGuire gets up jitterbugging steam with Private Ed Maron at New York's famed American Theater Wing's Stage Door Canteen. LIFE noted the servicemen's verdict on the Canteen: "No liquor, but damned good anyway."

LIFE and Private John Farnsworth, looking hot under the collar, went to a party thrown in Hollywood by not one, but eight movie lovelies (from left): Barbara Hale, Lynne Baggett, Gloria DeHaven, Lynn Bari, Jinx Falkenberg, Dolores Moran, Chili Williams and Ginger Rogers.

Not even GI longjohns can disguise the shapely Dietrich gams as Marlene peels off army boots and slips on gold pumps for a show she was getting ready to put on for U.S. troops. On one tour, she was often so close to the front lines that soldiers came to her performances toting rifles.

Wide-mouth comedian Joe E. Brown signs autographs for troops in the South Pacific. Brown's soldier son had been killed a few months earlier.

At Washington's National Press Club Canteen, Vice-President Harry Truman plays the "Missouri Waltz" for actress Lauren Bacall—and the boys.

Starlet Marie McDonald ankles downstairs on her way to a benefit show, outfitted as nurse. She and 99 other screen folk did a series of 12 one-night stands, covering 8,000 railroad miles and raising over $600,000 for Army and Navy relief.

The archetypal doughboy of World War I, composer Irving Berlin wraps a World War I puttee before launching into a quavery version of his unforgettable "Oh, How I Hate to Get Up in the Morning," the hit of his 1918 show, *Yip, Yip, Yaphank*. He stole his own show when he encored the number in his World War II allsoldier production, *This is the Army*.

181

War in the Air: the Battle of the Bombers

U.S. air chief Spaatz

Waist gunner

Bomber crews

Bombsight expert

Strategic air power—long-range bombing of the enemy's home territory and its war-making facilities, as distinct from tactical air power, which supported the advance of surface forces—came of age in World War II. For reasons of geography, it came to the European theater long before it arrived in the Pacific. The European continent was within the range of U.S. B-17 Flying Fortresses based in Britain, and within a year of Pearl Harbor, airmen in the insect-like gear of the high-altitude flier were operating from that "unsinkable carrier."

In the bombardment of the Continent, the U.S. Army Air Force was not alone. Britain's Halifaxes and Lancasters had started pounding Germany early in the war, beginning in 1940 with the bombing of the Ruhr's industrial cities. But the British and the Americans differed on how to go about strategic bombing. Losses had caused the R.A.F. to give up daylight attacks for nighttime area bombing. Protected by fighters, U.S. bombers carried out daylight attacks on specific targets from great altitudes using precision-bombing techniques made

Wrapped in sheepskin coats and wearing helmets, oxygen masks, and eye shades, two fliers of the Eighth Air Force were photographed by

over the Enemy Homeland

possible by America's closely guarded secret weapon, the Norden bombsight. The U.S. Eighth Air Force and the R.A.F.'s Bomber Command joined in the Combined Bomber Offensive, and by mid-1944, when the Luftwaffe had lost air superiority, their assaults had reached a peak.

For much of the war, the homeland of Japan was protected from bombing by thousands of miles of ocean and armed islands. To bomb it required the capture of a seemingly endless succession of forward bases and the development of

longer range bombers than the workhorse B-17s and B-24s.

The answer was the huge, long-range B-29 Superfort. While the amphibious war crept toward the Marianas, from which this giant could reach Japan, the first B-29s were based in the long-ignored China-Burma-India theater. On June 15, 1944, as U.S. forces were making their first Marianas attack at Saipan, Superforts from Calcutta bombed steel works on the island of Kyushu. It was the first time Japan had been bombed since the Doolittle raid of 1942.

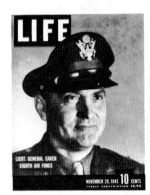

Daylight attacker Eaker

Night bomber Harris

Fighter escort

500-pound "eggs"

Margaret Bourke-White as they prepared for a high-altitude raid on Europe. The masks and the Norden bombsight made the raids possible.

183

Oily smoke billows over Ploesti, Rumania, as B-24s of the U.S. Ninth Air Force, based in North Africa, bomb oil refineries that were vital to Germany. The unescorted Liberators, which flew at tree-top level to escape radar detection and to duck under flak, put a crimp in Germany's oil supply and rocked its morale. But the raid cost 54 of 177 bombers, some of which had been transferred to Africa from the Eighth Air Force.

'Let's take it easy or somebody might get hurt'

Manning three cameras in a space less than the size of a phone booth, Frank Scherschel covered the massive September 6, 1943, daylight raid on Stuttgart in Winning Run, *an Eighth Air Force B-17 that was crippled but returned to crash-land on the English coast.*

"Tourist at 10 o'clock."

The first German fighter appeared, a speck out in the sky. He reminded me of a lone duck that refuses to be decoyed. It is an FW-190. One of our machine guns fires a short burst and the whole ship vibrates. At the same time my intercom goes out completely and when it comes on again our bombs are away and we are heading for home. Then fighters come from all directions.

"Fighter at 12 o'clock level . . . "

He came straight in, head on . . . I tried to take a picture but must have ducked too soon . . . .

About this time I ran out of film. Laboriously I climbed down into the hatch and sat down . . . a quick glance at the oxygen pressure—it was now down below 250. The little red ball was jumping up and down like a jumping jack. Opening the camera and extracting the film, I looked for a way to seal the gummed label. My oxygen mask covered my mouth and I didn't want to fool around taking it off for fear of not getting it back on properly. The problem was solved very simply—I just passed one finger over my sweating brow and there was enough moisture for three rolls of film. The guns are chattering away every few moments. Now I know what the communiqué means when it says the Forts fight their way back from the target. I had left my filters below in the nose of the plane. Getting confidence in the handling of my oxygen mask I change to a walk-around bottle and crawl down for my other camera and a filter. On the way back I hear a noise that sounds something like a siren. My intercom wasn't plugged in so I hadn't heard the conversation. Coming up the hatch I see a lot of lights flickering on the pilot's panel beneath the throttles of the ship. Our No. 3 motor is dead.

Pilot to navigator: "How soon do we meet our fighters?"

Navigator to pilot: "In about an hour."

Waist gunner to pilot: "Want us to lighten our load?"

The copilot takes off his mask and shouts at me. "Better go back to the radio room—take your chute."

I shed all my surplus gear and go down the hatch for my chute. Meet Lieutenant Scoggins throwing out ammunition, take time and help him. Lieutenant Witt, the bombardier, comes back with a heavy box of ammo. "Damn shame we couldn't shoot it at those fighters." Through the hatch between the engineer's legs I head through the bomb bay for the radio room. I try to squeeze through the catwalk but my heavy clothing and parachute harness stop me.

I go around and walk into what was a radio room. All the radio equipment

▲ Two heavy bombs drop toward German submarine pens, concrete U-boat shelters 12 feet thick, at Lorient on the coast of Brittany.

The Focke-Wulf plane factory at Marienburg in East Prussia lies riddled with bomb craters after a raid by U.S. heavy bombers. Britain's Air Chief Marshal Sir Charles Portal called the strike "the most perfect example in history of the accurate distribution of bombs over a target."

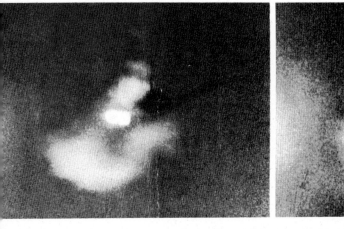

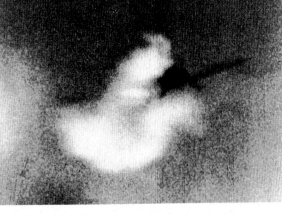

◄ The death of a Focke-Wulf fighter is recorded by the wing camera synchronized with an American Thunderbolt fighter escort's machine guns. Hit from astern, the FW-190's pilot's canopy splinters, the engine smokes and bursts into flame, and the blazing plane plummets earthward.

that was loose or could be pried loose was being thrown overboard. At the remaining radio a grim radioman is sending an S.O.S. The radioman stops and shouts, "We have reached the Channel, prepare to ditch." We take off our chutes and cut the safety wires of the rubber dinghies. We peek out of the hatch and look at the Channel. "Helluva lot better than Germany or France," somebody shouts. The radioman is still sending an S.O.S. He stops. We are not going to ditch.

"Prepare to bail out."

We snap on our chutes. Sergeant Hamilton comes over to me and looks over my harness and chute . . . puts his mouth to my ear: "Go out crouching like this. When you jump, go head first and count ten before you pull the ripcord."

We see the beautiful English coastline. The navigator has found an airport.

"Prepare to land in a small airport."

We all sit on the floor bracing our backs against the wall behind us. We are turning in. The flaps are down, the motors sound throttled completely (they were out). Martel, the radioman, is sitting in his armored chair and peeking out of a window. "Here we go," he shouts. The wheels hit with a bang. We bounce twice with more noise. Then there is a helluva lot of noise and we are all thrown up in the air and sideways. The plane has stopped. Nobody moves. Somebody says, "Let's get the hell out of here. . . ." Sergeant Hamilton says, "Let's take it easy or somebody might get hurt. . . ."

Everyone slowed down and we got the hell out of there. Our tail surfaces were in a hedge and we ran around the wing. Lieutenant James saw us, counted noses. Everybody was out.

Safely back in England, the *Winning Run* crew pose on their pancaked B-17's wing.

Flying Fortresses, and maybe secret intelligence, win the Battle

# of Bismarck Sea

A B-17 skip-bombs a Japanese freighter in an Alexander Leydenfrost drawing. LIFE used it to illustrate its story of the "miracle" Allied Air Forces Commander Lieutenant General George C. Kenney had wrought in sinking 22 enemy ships in the Bismarck Sea. The official release said a B-24 had spotted the convoy. But some historians credit the Ultra cryptographic machine, which had revealed enemy codes.

Chilly air warden

Price boss Henderson

Tribulations Back Home

In the small towns and the cities, on the farms and in the factories, Americans became aware that war was changing their lives. Wages were higher, but butter was up to 46 cents a pound. The work could be hard and the hours atrocious as war plants went on round-the-clock shifts. Trains were dirty and crowded—travel was discouraged if not restricted. Shortages of fuel, food and clothing ruined vacations, Sunday dinners and the simple pleasures of dressing up. Worst of all, families were painfully separated or uprooted as fathers, sons and lovers were called to war.

Yet when all the gripes were in, Americans—compared with Britons or Chinese, for example—had it pretty easy. The war was a nuisance, sometimes a miserably anxious one, but not real hardship. LIFE recorded the irritations and other shifts of mood and activity regularly, partly because they made lively stories, but also because they gave GIs some assurance that the people at home missed them, that they were doing their best for the "war effort," and that despite some strains and dislocations, the important things would all be there when the fighting men came home.

Widowed Mrs. Julia Braun of Hamilton, Ohio, sits mending in her chair by the window. Above her hangs a single blue star, which symbolizes that a man of the house is in the service—in her case an only son in Iran.

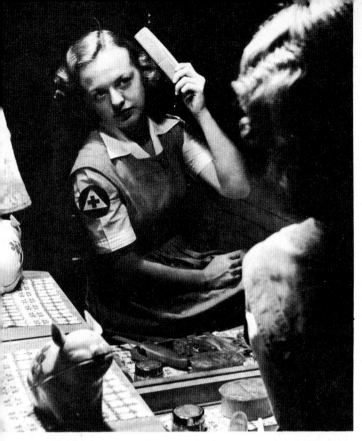

Janet Fritz, popular and pretty native of Hamilton, Ohio, where she was discovered by Alfred Eisenstaedt, gets ready for her stint as a volunteer nurses' aide. At night, like many other young women, she gave up free time to help out in a hospital that had lost much of its staff to the war.

Matt Thomson, a Hamilton YMCA secretary, takes over the mothering chores to liberate his wife for an evening out. Before the war, capable baby sitters had been easy to find; now the Thomsons were dependent on inexperienced girls—or forced to take turns at the job themselves.

Lois Bardwell of Indianapolis waits for her boyfriend, Bill Eder, to come back from the war. The door to the Eder family car is open, ready for Bill to slide in and take the wheel. LIFE ran this picture, along with others on the Eder family, in an issue called "A Letter to GIs."

"Don't Travel!" said LIFE, showing as an example of the hazards of wartime junketing this picture by Ed Clark of a jammed Southern Railway coach. Top-priority troop movements and servicemen on furlough packed the trains, and civilians were urged not to complicate the problem.

Some determined citizens regulate the tightening of

BOARD

American belts

These are not the enemy—although many people thought of them that way. They are the members of the Bristol. Connecticut. Ration Board who were described in LIFE as "friendly but firm" as they regulated the menus of civilians for the Office of Price Administration.

U.S. production hits an all-time peak

By the spring of 1944, U.S. assembly lines were operating at full pitch in response to the demands—and the gigantic waste—of modern war. In the three years that followed Pearl Harbor, the country's war plants cranked out a staggering 220 million tons of steel and were now producing at a rate of 90 million tons per year. The U.S. had also built 202,000 planes; 59,000 boats and ships; 380,000 big guns, and 12 million machine guns, rifles and carbines. The total cost: $191 billion.

The factory worker had become as much a part of the war as the soldier. Working against shortages of fuel and raw materials, Americans toiled 24 hours a day on oil rigs and in automobile factories converted to tank assembly lines. More than 225,000 workers produced munitions in plants that had once produced Kodaks and Cokes. And despite an influx of unskilled labor, production climbed steadily as industrial techniques improved. Airplanes, long the product of a few loving hands, now came off the assembly line, and shipyard tasks that had taken 100 man-hours in 1941 were accomplished in 45 man-hours by the mid-1940s. And it all seemed to be paying off—at home as well as abroad. As good news from the war fronts grew from a trickle to a stream, absenteeism plummeted. The industrial payroll rose from $13 billion in 1939 to $44 billion in 1944, and full employment put an end—at last—to the Great Depression.

◄ Andreas Feininger's depiction of industrial might—a plant in McKeesport, Pennsylvania—ran in an issue on wartime America.

Five-hundred-pound bombs hang ► like sausages on the conveyor line in Feininger's picture of the A.O. Smith plant in Milwaukee.

The 5,000th Boeing B-17 rolls off a Seattle assembly line into a crowd of the proud workers who built her. Their names cover her fuselage.

The burning hull of the troopship *Lafayette*, launched as the *Normandie*, lists heavily in New York City's icy Hudson River. Sabotage was suspected, but it later proved to be negligence—sparks from a worker's acetylene torch ignited kapok mattresses stored in a lounge.

Montgomery Ward President Sewall Avery is removed from his premises by the U.S. Army. Because he had refused to comply with a War Labor Board order that required him to include a "maintenance-of-membership" clause in the union contract, the government took over his plant.

Mistakes and squabbles flaw the war effort

Defeats and reverses at home, though seldom a matter of life and death as they were on the battlefronts, often made spectacular picture-stories. Sometimes the home-front losses turned up as the result of plain carelessness, as when the French liner *Normandie* caught fire in 1942 *(left)* just as she had been converted into a troopship. A long-term defeat was the bitter legacy of race riots in cities like Detroit, where black and white Americans mauled and murdered each other in 1943, and the only winner, LIFE pointed out, was Hitler.

Strikes and other labor disputes represented a particularly troublesome wartime setback. Of such incidents, perhaps one of the oddest was the controversy, over a manager's refusal to recognize a union, that ended as shown below. LIFE chided the U.S. government for not exhausting all legal remedies before resorting to "violence"—but acknowledged that the victim had suffered only a "synthetic martyrdom."

Penn Station goodbye

Life Goes Back to Pennsylvania Station

Boys and girls say their tender, sad goodbys, unmindful of their part in a great, familiar drama

112

by a master of the candid camera

The look of New York's Pennsylvania Station has changed since Alfred Eisenstaedt took pictures there last spring (LIFE, April 19). Then first goodbys were being said. Today they are a different kind—those of boys and girls who have said goodby many times by now. They stand in front of the gates leading to the trains, deep in each other's arms, not caring who sees or what they think. Each goodby is a drama complete in itself, which Eisenstaedt's pictures movingly tell. Sometimes the girl stands with arms around the boy's waist, hands tightly clasped behind. Another fits her head into the curve of his cheek while tears fall onto his coat. Now and then the boy will take her face between his hands and speak reassuringly. Or if the wait is long they may just stand quietly, not saying anything. The common denominator of all these goodbys is sadness and tenderness, and complete oblivion for the moment to anything but their own individual heartaches.

CONTINUED ON NEXT PAGE

1943-1944

The Bleak Aleutians

The volcanic Aleutian islands, a treeless, uninhabited world of instant fogs, 100-mile winds, sharply tilted landscapes and horizontal rains, were a terrifying war theater. Tough Japanese defenders occupied Attu, the outermost Aleutian island. They had seized it, along with neighboring Kiska, in an abortive 1942 campaign that was designed to lure the U.S. Pacific Fleet north.

In the Aleutians the frigid Bering Sea meets the warm Pacific in cyclonic swirls of fog. The Japanese on Attu dug into mountainsides, let the Americans land and remained concealed. They waited in the fog until the advancing riflemen became visible and then fired. On rare clear days, they could be located in their foxholes, but they seldom surrendered. In the end, it was the Japanese high command that gave up. An August landing on Kiska found that the entire occupying force had been evacuated under cover of fog.

On Adak, an Aleutian island air base, a bomber crew plays poker in a Quonset hut decorated from floor to ceiling with pin-ups. Confined by gales and rain, Adak GIs went stir-crazy. Most entertainers missed Adak; exceptions were actress Maria Ouspenskaya and Jinx Falkenberg.

U.S. troops, their pup tents and some early supplies dot the tundra of an Attu beach during the unopposed first phase of their landing.

Two Americans peer cautiously at the dead defenders of a dugout. Of 2,500 Japanese on Attu, at least 1,791 died and only 11 were captured.

In the smoke of exploding grenades, a U.S. squad moves in to mop up Japanese dugouts. In the tundra of the coast and lower mountain slopes, the Japanese occupiers had elaborately interconnected their dugouts with tunnels, enabling them to move unseen—in some cases for miles. ▼

Soldiers from an isolated outpost are carted to a movie by means of a tractor and a tracked trailer. The viscous mud under the sedge of Attu's tundra was as much as eight feet deep and so sodden that in wet weather "cat" trains like this would push bow-waves ahead of them. ▼

Chili Williams, "The Polka-Dot Girl," appeared first in a letters column, and returned several times by popular demand, full-page size.

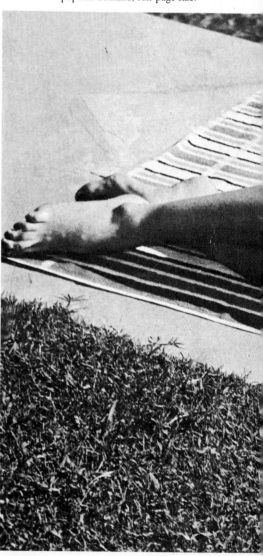

Contender for the most famous pin-up of all time is LIFE's 1941 picture of Rita Hayworth, taken by Bob Landry, who alternated such assignments in Hollywood with combat photography in the Pacific, Italy and France. GI response to this photograph was usually a simple "Wow!"

A Pin-up Portfolio

Never blind to the charms of pretty girls in peacetime, LIFE's editors perceived a pleasant duty when war came. They rallied around to meet the needs of a new kind of reader—the lonely male in uniform—and published some of the most famous pictures ever taken. Photographs such as those shown here generated a gratifying response. Within 60 days after he had submitted a photograph of Chili Williams *(left)* to a LIFE letters column, model agent Harry Conover was swamped with more than 10,000 requests for copies, and Chili (who is now a California housewife and mother of two grown children) went to Hollywood *(page 179).*

Though the pictures were basically intended for pin-up display, the editors saw it as part of their duty to back up the artwork with solid information. Readers were told that "Miss Williams is 21 years old . . . waist 24 inches, bust 34 inches. . . . Her gray-blue eyes are like limpid pools." In the editors' minds, the grueling hours they spent assembling articles about such young women were amply rewarded by the knowledge that their sweet, sexy faces and figures were essential equipment on barracks walls in every military outpost around the world *(pages 198–199).*

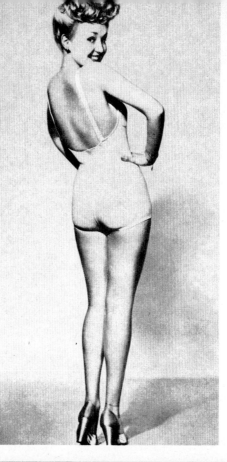

Betty Grable became Mrs. Harry James shortly after posing for this picture, also a candidate for most famous pin-up. Her marital status did not prevent hundreds of thousands of servicemen from decorating their quarters with her likeness.

In an early, intensive survey of Army posts, LIFE found that pin-ups of sultry Dorothy Lamour, who was already off on her endless *Road* series with Bing Crosby and Bob Hope, outnumbered all others by 3 to 1.

1943-1944

"Vinegar Joe" Stilwell

Flying Tiger boss Chennault

CBI: Forgotten Arena

Having seized Malaya, the Japanese moved on Burma, through which—via the Burma Road *(page 204)*—lay China's only access to her allies. Alarmed, Generalissimo Chiang Kai-shek sent three Chinese armies under his American Chief of Staff, Major General Joseph Stilwell, to reinforce the thin British colonial forces defending Burma. Also on the scene was Claire Chennault, who in 1941 had recruited Army, Navy and Marine fliers into his Flying Tigers.

The Tigers, who painted their old Curtiss P-40s like sharks, consistently bested the faster Japanese Zeros. But the Japanese ground forces cut swiftly through the jungle to Rangoon, Burma's only major port. After a punishing retreat back to China, "Vinegar Joe" Stilwell bluntly told the world: "We got a hell of a beating."

The loss of Burma meant that all China's supplies had to be flown in over the Hump *(page 205)*, and reconquest of Burma was clearly necessary. But in planning it, ground commander Stilwell collided with Chennault, who saw China-Burma-India primarily as an air theater. Both suffered frustration: Chiang refused to commit Chinese armies unless Britain provided craft for amphibious attack on Burma. Britain chose to conduct its naval campaign and the U.S. sent most of its planes to fight in the central Pacific. The result: a three-year stalemate in the CBI.

Three of the few Japanese tanks in Burma, eight-year-old 14-tonners with horse-drawn transport, pass a wrecked British ambulance.

A Flying Tiger prepares to take off in his P-40 from a field north of Rangoon. In one dogfight, Tigers downed 20 of 78 Japanese and lost none.

◄ Indian troops of the Burma Frontier Force, under cover of riflemen, board a sampan to carry the war to the enemy across the Sittang River.

Thousands of Chinese laborers, using picks, shovels and muscle, prepare an airstrip in rugged Hunan province for ▼ Chennault's fliers. Stilwell believed airfield building should await the buildup of ground forces to protect them. Only weeks after this field was completed, the Japanese overran it.

▲ Southeast Asia's most successful commander. Lieutenant General Tomoyuki Yamashita, inspects captured ruins. He had studied Germany's 1940 European campaigns at first hand and conquered Singapore and Bataan. He defended the Philippines against MacArthur in 1945.

Two ways over the Hump: the hard way and the harder

Supply trucks dot the hairpin undulations of the Burma Road. The Chinese built the tortuous mountain link between Kunming and the Burmese railhead of Lashio in 1938. The Japanese demanded that the British close the road in 1940, but had to invade Burma and shut it themselves.

The Mekong River winds its way through a tropical valley whose steep sides plunge from the Hump—snow-capped 20,000-foot heights of the Himalayas. Contrasts of heat and humidity caused perpetual mists and treacherous air currents that could make Hump-flying C-47s rise or fall 1,500 feet in seconds. Hump pilots also faced Japanese air opposition, but still managed to haul 60,000 tons of strategic matériel monthly.

The Marauders and the Chindits wind it up in Burma

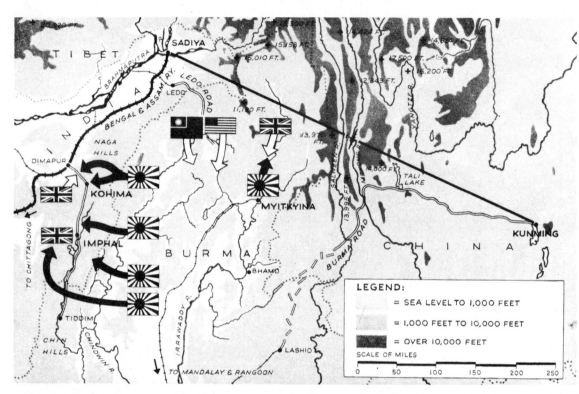

Moves that capped 1943–1944 action in the CBI are mapped at left. Allied units pushing towards the Burma Road gateway of Myitkyina were spurred by the exploits of irregular troops—British Major General Orde C. Wingate's Chindits (named after a winged beast in Burmese myth) and U.S. Major General Frank Merrill's Marauders. To the west, the Japanese threatened the railroad supplying the Hump airlift, and made a serious—but unsuccessful—bid to invade India. The August 4, 1944, capture of Myitkyina threatened Japanese rear units, and sped their eventual defeat.

The campaign winds up on a Myitkyina airfield captured by the Marauders. Bernard Hoffman, who had been with them, photographed a fallen Japanese and a C-47 landing. Strafed by Zeros, another C-47 burns.

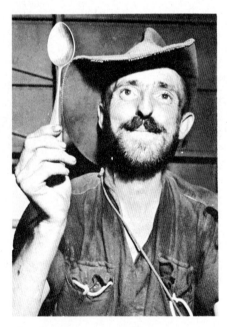

Jim Rogerson, one of Wingate's Chindits who walked 170 miles through enemy-held jungle after being cut off without supplies, displays the column's only spoon, which was used to mix an occasional batch of biscuits.

A patrol of Merrill's Marauders sweeps a jungle trail to protect the main column. The Marauders traveled light, discarding even mess gear, except for a cup and spoon.

Sailor boy meets girl

All's Fair in Wartime Love

"A soldier boy without a heart has two strikes on him from the start," said Irving Berlin's wartime hit from *This Is the Army.* LIFE endorsed the sentiment. Week after week "Life Goes to a Party" introduced readers to soldiers, sailors, Marines and airmen meeting, partying, dating and marrying the girls they fell in love with. Photographers followed servicemen from rowboats in New York's Central Park to gondolas in the Vale of Kashmir to show that love and marriage had not been banished by war.

Soldiers on furlough from the front and sailors on liberty in ports from Casablanca to Newport News found girls to meet and court—WAACs, Wrens and Red Cross nurses, pretty Englishwomen and lovely locals at far-flung bases, even the girl next door. The dates were mostly bittersweet, brief diversions very different from the relationships cemented at the prewar corner drugstore or the movie palace. Though now and then quick familiarity bred love and a wartime wedding, the pictures were poignant evidence that the upheavals of the times were irreversible, and that the old boy-meets-girl patterns would never be the same again.

Palmer Hoyt III, a United Press correspondent, takes Barbara Stephens of the U.S. Information Service for a sedan-chair ride in Chungking.

Memphis Belle pilot Robert K. Morgan sweeps up an armful of his own Memphis belle, Margaret Polk, for whom the famed B-17 was named.

On leave from Pacific combat duty, Navy pilot John Sullivan had just wed Mary Loretta Desmarai in Springfield, Massachusetts.

Alfred Eisenstaedt photographed Yeoman Frederick Witham and Pauline Hatfield at their New York civil marriage ceremony.

Corporal and Mrs. Joseph Le Bash enjoy the California sun with their baby. Mrs. Le Bash met her husband in her native Australia.

On a sailor's holiday, Seaman Therrl Heiselman grins as New York schoolgirl Ann Barbarett hugs him in a rowboat on Central Park lake.

Football hero Tommy Harmon admires Elyse Knox in her weddinggown material—the parachute he wore when shot down over China.

Wistful honeymooners Edna and Marine pilot Marion Carl cling to each other and the last days of his Oregon home leave.

Marine William Baldwin and young actress Kim Hunter are wed in Hollywood. They had known each other just two months before marriage.

In a boat named *Careless Rapture*, Lieutenant Vaden Carney and British censor Pamela Rumbold glide on a canal in India's Vale of Kashmir.

1943-1944

Flier and son

Brief Respite

The sailor was home from the sea and the soldier was back from the war—only a few, and usually only for a matter of days. While the leaves lasted, old men gathered to hear tales of recent battles; children listened, entranced, as older pilot brothers told of dog-fights; and women wept, exhausted from their hopes and anxieties.

For the too-brief moment, men at war could taste the pleasures of peace. Ovens warmed with apple pies for them; ration points were squandered on their favorite dishes; frilly, sexy nightgowns were best sellers, at prices that were outrageous even in those days.

LIFE reported on the homecomings with a little cheesecake and a lot of compassion, following sailors into small-town kitchens, soldiers into comfortable parlors (where they could tell and retell their stories), capturing the sense of fleeting joy that furloughs brought.

The GI's furlough dream involved sexy lingerie, and LIFE indulged it with a story on "Furlough Nighties," which featured this black number.

Joe Moe tells oldtimers in his hometown of Tioga, North Dakota, how he was wounded at Guadalcanal with the 164th Infantry Regiment.

Sixteen lonely months of separation dissolve in tears of joy as Mrs. Bob Moore sees her Army husband greet their little girl.

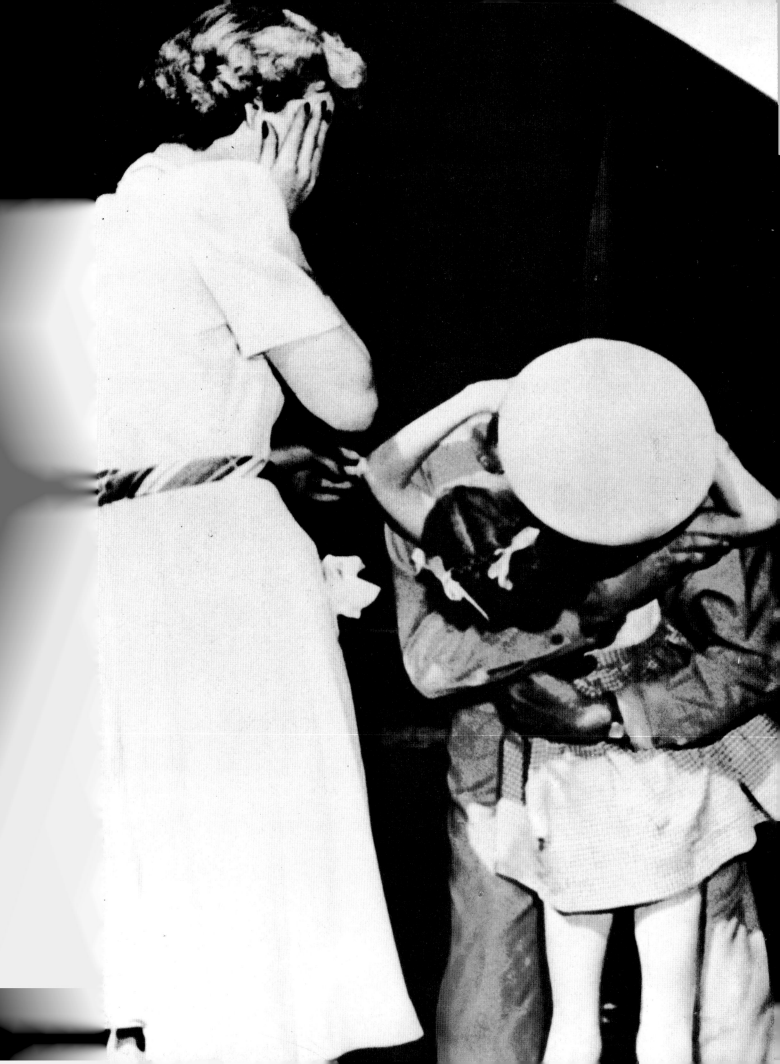

1943-1944

Ashore in Italy

Landing in Sicily

Just before midnight on July 9, 1943, Allied forces opened the first campaign of the war against the enemy on his own soil. Led by U.S. parachute and glider troops, they took the Italians and Germans by surprise and landed on the island of Sicily, just across the narrow Strait of Messina from the toe of mainland Italy's boot. Wind blew some of the invaders off their objectives, and the rallying defenders repelled them from some target airfields. But soon infantrymen, landed by a fleet of new amphibious landing craft, had seized the island's southeastern tip.

The Italian townspeople—and even their soldiers—appeared eager to have Mussolini and the Germans driven out. Though Italian soldiers gave up by the thousands, the Germans resisted stubbornly. The British under General Montgomery raced General Patton's Americans to Messina, battling up the coast around the 10,705-foot volcano, Mount Etna. Patton, whose western route via Palermo was easier, barely got to Messina ahead of Monty. But when the Americans arrived, they found that the Germans had brilliantly ferried 109,000 troops with equipment to the mainland to fight again.

Italian prisoners, carrying little more than clothing, are marched through the surf to be loaded onto an infantry landing craft for evacuation.

In an amazingly lifelike model by designer Norman Bel Geddes, engineers start to repair bomb damage at a secured airfield.

The town of Monreale gives a big hand to GIs rolling through on their way to Palermo. In such towns the only thing they had to defend against was young Sicilians hitching rides.

A rag-clad Sicilian, with the First Division's Brigadier General Theodore Roosevelt, gestures in the local equivalent of "They went thataway."

A medical corpsman of the U.S. Seventh Army gets a shoeshine in Palermo while another soldier, in no particular hurry, waits in line. At Licata, where troops first landed, AMGOT, the Allied Military Government of Occupied Territory, went into action. John Hersey cabled LIFE a report about it, which was later the basis of his novel, play and film, *A Bell for Adano*.

Up the boot on foot

Operation Avalanche: Invasion of Italy

Down the Italian boot from Naples, the mountains familiar to generations of tourists end in miles of curving beaches that rim the Gulf of Salerno. The only flatland within range of Allied fighter planes on newly won Sicily, it was an obvious target for an invasion. When General Mark Clark's Fifth Army hit the Salerno beaches in Operation Avalanche, the German Army was well entrenched there.

In the five days before the September 9, 1943, landing, the British Eighth Army had crossed the Messina Straits, landed on the toe and worked its way from Reggio to the Adriatic port of Bari high on the heel. Discredited by this landing, by African defeats and by the fall of Sicily, Mussolini's Fascist government collapsed, and its successor capitulated to the Allies. But this political reverse did nothing whatsoever to deter the Germans that were waiting at Salerno with zeroed-in artillery and panzers behind miles of minefields and strong points.

Assaulting the beach from the left, British Commandos and U.S. Rangers slipped ashore to seize the passes behind the Amalfi Drive hills that led to Naples. Salerno's airfield was taken in two days, but German guns, firing from high in the hills, rendered it unusable. Mountain warfare had begun in a country that is essentially two mountain ranges: the Alps and the Apennines, separated by the Po valley. By October 1, 1943, the Allies had driven through to Naples, which the Nazis left in ruins. Between the city and the Po lay hundreds of miles of German-held mountains; Clark chose to move on Rome before challenging the Apennines. Through the fall and winter the Allies clawed their way to the Rapido River, where they were halted by the enemy atop Monte Cassino, and reached Rome only in June.

Amphibious war bursts over the Gulf of Salerno in this LIFE drawing. German shells rip the beaches and explode among landing craft that are only partially protected by destroyer-laid smoke screens.

Youthful anti-Fascist snipers (the cigarette-smoking youngest is nine) surfaced when the fleeing Germans razed parts of Naples. The Nazis had a particular hatred for Naples, and committed atrocities on its landscape, culture and people that left Neapolitans embittered for years.

Robert Capa photographed a knot of wailing Neapolitan women mourning sons who were killed in the resistance. Twenty boys from one school were killed in the guerrilla fighting.

Cassino and its monastery are pulverized, but stubborn Germans

still bar the road to Rome

Smoke rises from the ruins of Cassino after a March 1944 attack by artillery and waves of bombers. The action climaxed 10 weeks of futile blasting of the town. At the upper right is Castle Hill, held by the Allies; below it is German-held Hill 165. The Rapido is in the foreground.

1943-1944

Anzio: the Allies lose a costly gamble

One of the most controversial operations of the war in Italy, code-named Shingle, sought to outflank the Germans plugging the bottleneck at Cassino by an amphibious landing on the coast at Anzio, more than 60 miles to the west. Enthusiastically supported by Winston Churchill, it was a brilliant gamble, but it failed disastrously. Though Allied troops on the main Cassino front were stalled, the British and Americans landed at Anzio with relatively little resistance and proceeded some 10 miles inland toward a line of hills. Field Marshal Kesselring quickly brought in some six divisions, including the elite Hermann Göring Division, from northern Italy, France, Yugoslavia and Germany itself. Then, pouring fire and hurling armor from the hills, they pushed the Allies back.

The Anzio invaders, ceding the high ground to the Germans as they had at Cassino, remained trapped on a sea-level wedge, 10 miles long and 10 miles deep, that they could neither enlarge nor abandon. Although Kesselring was unable to drive them into the sea—the Allies retained naval and air superiority—he advanced as far as their final beachhead line, beyond which the Allied commander, Major General John P. Lucas, had ordered no retreat. For three months artillery pounded the shallow beachhead, and the weary infantry, despite the numbers of the killed and wounded, held on until they were reinforced with enough strength to breach the hills and become part of the big May breakthrough to Rome.

LSTs unload fresh American troops in Anzio harbor to reinforce holders of a beachhead smashed by months of German artillery pounding.

White puffs of smoke from 4.2-inch chemical mortars start a smoke screen to mask the advance of beachhead forces toward higher ground.

At Anzio George Silk pictured Private First Class Robert Scullion of Salem, Ohio, with the Purple Heart he was awarded for a wound he received while in the beachhead hospital. Invalided for stomach trouble, he was hit when shell fragments ripped his ward tent.

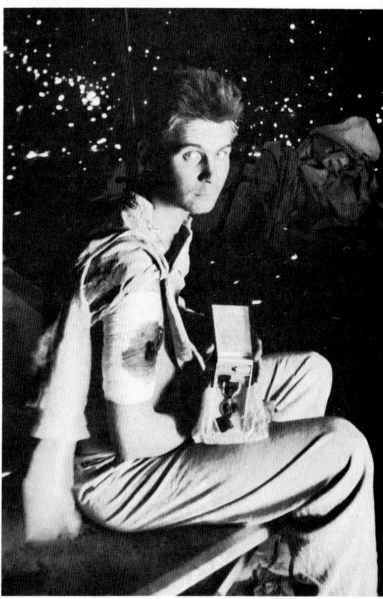

Germans surrender to Allied forces moving toward Rome in May 1944 after the fall of Cassino, which was taken by the Polish Corps.

General Mark Clark rides past St. Peter's with two of his divisional commanders as his Fifth Army enters Rome on June 4, two days before the Normandy invasion.

'I tried to convince Hitler'

Right after the Allied landings in Italy, Mussolini was deposed and placed under arrest. Though guarded by 250 men on a mountain top in the Abruzzi, he was rescued, on Hitler's orders, by a paratroop commando unit under SS Lieutenant Otto Skorzeny and brought to Germany. Ironically, before his rescue he had complained bitterly about his German ally to Admiral Franco Maugeri, head of Italian naval intelligence, who took the following notes that appeared in LIFE:

Never have the Germans understood the importance of the Mediterranean. I told them early in the war that it was necessary to occupy Egypt; subsequently we would have joined the Middle East with the East. Already they had had the godsend of defeating the French army in a spectacularly short time. And what did they do? They went and set up a Russian front! And this, after winning the political battle of the "alliance" [the Russo-German Pact], which they snatched right under the noses of the British, who had been on watch against just such an alliance for more than five months.

They maintain that Russia is a very serious danger to Western civilization. I tried to convince Hitler that this is an obsession. Hitler does not understand that Stalin has killed Bolshevism by putting to death first-rate men. Stalin has given up the idea of a world revolution. But it is useless to tell Hitler this. He is still anchored to his old beliefs.

I was the first to recognize Soviet Russia. I asked Litvinov to come to Rome. We signed a friendship pact. The Germans had thought they could liquidate Russia in a few months. They were diabolically deceived by the Russians. The Russian mobilization plan was offered to the German intelligence service. But it was all faked. Where it mentioned 50 cavalry brigades, it should have read 50 armored brigades, and so on.

I advised Hitler to come to some agreement with Russia. I tried to play on his superstition. I reminded him that his first Russian campaign in 1941 did not succeed. Then I asked him to remember that terrible first winter. Then I mentioned the disaster at Stalingrad. But it was no good. I told him: "You must make peace with Russia. You must bring all your forces into the Mediterranean. You cannot help us now, not because you do not want to, but because you cannot unless you make peace with Russia." But it was no good.

A defeated Mussolini flees to a loyal colleague.

When Hitler declared war, I gained nine months of peace for Italy with my formula of nonbelligerence. Then I had to intervene. Otherwise we should have had to renounce every chance of bringing France to satisfactory terms. As for me, I was sure then that the Germans would land victoriously in England, where they (the British) had only 200 bronze cannons in all! Perhaps a landing would not have driven the British to surrender—they might have transferred their government to Canada or Australia—but we would have had formidable positions.

Gibraltar? That also I suggested to Hitler. He replied that he was not sure of Franco's position. We should have told Franco we were going to pass over his territory with or without his permission.

The Guerrillas

Wherever Hitler set his conquering foot, bands of patriots sprang up to harry his legions and repay ruthlessness with death. In Russia, guerrillas were a continuing threat, and the *maquis* in France and *partigiani* in Italy were no less so. In Greece, partisans tied up thousands of German troops that were badly needed elsewhere. Nowhere did a guerrilla movement produce an army better disciplined than in Yugoslavia, where a Marxist former metalworker named Josip Broz, known as Tito, whipped farmers, city workers and students into a liberation army. In two years of fighting they were converted from a rabble to a smoothly meshed fighting force that won back much of their native land before the Allies brought liberation. In Greece, guerrillas of the Greek Sacred Squadron were accompanied by LIFE artist Bernard Perlin and correspondent Percy Knauth as they ranged the occupied Aegean islands. As part of a combined British-Greek force they waged a stealthy, merciless war.

A Greek guerrilla officer and a partisan reservist join townspeople of a propartisan village in listening to BBC news on a German radio. Behind them is a priest; others are ▲ wounded guerrillas, mothers and children. Artist Perlin visited the village with a guerrilla contingent.

Tito was photographed by LIFE's John Phillips in his headquarters cave in Yugoslavia. His dog, Tigar, was captured from a German.

A guerrilla band bears off a British ▶ Marine, his foot shattered by a grenade. The band lost their fight and fled to avoid instigating reprisals.

In a seaside hospital, the wounded Briton's gangrenous leg is amputated. Perlin told of "the stink of decayed flesh, thick blood, ether. . . ." ▼

Townspeople bring flowers to the amputee in his hospital bed. Local women kept a 24-hour vigil, Perlin reported, and the Marine grew

stronger, although his leg was slow to heal. To permit drainage, no flap of skin had been drawn over the stump. He was taken to Turkey, then home.

Spencer Tracy, a ghost pilot visible only to the audience, helps trainee flier Van Johnson through a tough maneuver in *A Guy Named Joe*.

Raymond Massey glares, a vision of ▶ Nazi evil, in *Desperate Journey*. Japanese villains were harder to cast: no one wanted to play them.

The crew of Hitchcock's *Lifeboat* battles a storm. The film drew criticism because its Nazi villain was the only practical man aboard.

Survivors, Nöel Coward in the foreground, cling to a life raft. The movie, *In Which We Serve*, was made with help from the Royal Navy.

A Hollywood Cast of Heroes and Villains

Hero-actor Murphy

Hollywood had a field day proving that war was hell. Here was the perfect excuse for blood, guts and lots of action on screen. Back lots were turned into battlegrounds, indoor tanks were awash with rolling prop ships, and the biggest stars—Gable, Tracy, Johnson—played the biggest heroes, when the heroes themselves weren't taking the roles *(right)*.

LIFE's reports on the war were a source for several of the Hollywood battle epics. Correspondent Melville Jacoby's pictures of the last days of Corregidor and Bataan were copied for *So Proudly we Hail.* Sergeant Al Schmid's story, *The Pride of the Marines (page 136),* drew heavily on LIFE's coverage of the Guadalcanal hero.

The moviegoing public swarmed to all of these gun operas, and money rolled into movie company coffers. Not all the films were made solely for theater audiences or studio gain. Walt Disney's huge animation outfit turned almost entirely to cartoon instruction films for the armed forces, and all the studios reeled forth educational and psychological warfare films on government order.

But film audiences got by far the biggest lift from the old Hollywood standbys—big moneymakers like *Mrs. Miniver* and *A Guy Named Joe,* and the slapstick antics of Bob Hope and Charlie Chaplin—or British films like Nöel Coward's hymn to the Royal Navy, *In Which We Serve.* Civilians and servicemen alike saw themselves glorified onscreen in the heart-tuggers, laughed at the ridiculous side of a dogface's sad-sack life and drew courage and resolve from many of the quasi-realistic, down-to-earth accounts of Everyman at war.

Medal of Honor winner Audie Murphy holds off two German infantry companies and five tanks in his own film story. *To Hell and Back.*

Lana Turner clings to Clark Gable in *Homecoming,* a film Gable made in 1948 after his own homecoming from three years' service in the Air Force.

227

'The Axis' stages a comic summit

One of the most famous meetings of the Axis partners took place not in the Brenner Pass but in Hollywood, and the leading characters were impersonated. Adolf Hitler's double was Charlie Chaplin, who in his 83rd film was playing the role of "Adenoid Hynkel" in *The Great Dictator*. His opposite number was Jack Oakie in the role of "Benzini Napaloni," a tyrant in the mold of Mussolini. In the scene at right, the status-conscious dictators are upstaging each other by raising barber chairs ever higher until they reach the ceiling.

Released before Pearl Harbor, *Dictator* immediately involved Chaplin in political controversy when U.S. Senate isolationists charged the movie industry and its "foreign born" (meaning British and Jewish) bosses with inciting the nation to war through films like *Convoy*, *Sergeant York* and *The Great Dictator*. Controversy came to LIFE over the secrecy with which Chaplin surrounded his masterpiece. Though no publicity pictures were permitted without his approval, LIFE's Hollywood reporter, Dick Pollard, managed to send the editors a purloined portrait of Chaplin-Hynkel-Hitler. But Pollard warned that Charlie might sue, and he did. In the only such crisis in LIFE's history, a judge ordered the magazine not to publish until it destroyed the Chaplin picture. Despite the suit, LIFE reported on the film—and published much more on the beloved Tramp in the years to come.

Hynkel-Hitler meets Napaloni-Mussolini in a barber shop.

Exhausted sergeant James Whitmore looks skyward for help in *Battleground*, a realistic 1949 movie about the Battle of the Bulge.

Five Graves to Cairo brought back one-time director Erich von Stroheim, "the man you love to hate," as Field Marshal Erwin Rommel.

Bob Hope, a movie star "draftee who faints at the sight of blood," mugs Hopishly from a shellhole through a mask of mud in *Caught in the Draft.*

An eerily accurate Hitler look-alike, actor Robert Watson drops to the ground during a violent moment in Hollywood's *The Hitler Gang.*

Frontline Funnies

"I can't be funny about the war," said 23-year-old frontline artist Sergeant Bill Mauldin in LIFE, "but I can try to make something out of the humorous situations which always accompany misery." And somehow he and a few of the nation's best cartoonists did produce hundreds of bitingly funny comments on life at the front. Mauldin's own Willie and Joe, appearing muddy, unshaven and exhausted in *Stars and Stripes*, were the most lifelike of the cartoon army. Their stripped-down humor drew shocked reactions from some of the brass, but the men under fire loved them. Of his drawings that ribbed the commissioned ranks, Mauldin said, "I never worry about hurting the feelings of the good officers when I draw officer cartoons. I build a shoe, and if somebody wants to put it on and loudly announce that it fits, that's his own affair."

Other favorites of the dogfaces were George Baker's tragicomic "Sad Sack," David Breger's well-meaning GI loser—who stumbled out of the pages of the enlisted men's weekly *Yank*—and the lovely Miss Lace of Milton Caniff's strip "Male Call," which appeared in thousands of local Army-post newspapers. From time to time, because they were such good cartoons and because they often gave an insight into the war that readers could not have gotten anywhere else, LIFE delightedly published selections from them all.

Lace called enlisted men "General" and preferred them to officers.

Lace spent a lot of time fending off amorous servicemen. LIFE admiringly called her "a magnificent figure of a girl."

"BEAUTIFUL VIEW! IS THERE ONE FOR THE ENLISTED MEN?"

"OH, I *LIKES* OFFICERS. THEY MAKE ME WANT TO LIVE TILL TH' WAR'S OVER."

Typical Mauldin humor was in the barbed cartoons above at right, but his own favorite was the old cavalryman shooting his jeep.

Grimly hapless, Mauldin's dogface Joe digs a foxhole in Italian rock.

Utterly helpless, George Baker's Sad Sack was a victim of the brass.

Truly hopeless, Dave Breger's private brings back the "enemy."

"OBJECTIVE"

The Sad Sack never won; his chief talent was making it in the face of awful odds—only to find survival wasn't worth it.

Private Breger really tried, and usually failed. He was so popular he stayed in *Yank* even when his creator became a lieutenant.

1943-1944
Yanks in England

A friendly army of Americans invaded Britain in the early 1940s. LIFE followed their progress from country cricket pitch to the occasional Sunday softball game in Hyde Park. For the most part, GIs were required to keep a low profile, and they generally kept strictly to themselves and did what they came to do—bomb Germany and prepare to invade it.

But the British knew why they were there and, when the Yanks did occasionally go on leave, treated them with respect and affection. As guests in Britain the Americans found they had to learn a whole new language: a streetcar was a "tram," cookies were "biscuits," a wrench a "spanner" and a bum not a derelict, but the human rear end. From time to time, customs caused some culture shock. LIFE's "How to Behave in England" essay pointed out that the British took a dim view of eager GIs who tried to strike up conversations with strangers on trains or in pubs. Baseball remained as much a mystery to the British as cricket was to the Yanks. The miracle was that an armed force, which at its peak numbered close to three million soldiers, sailors and airmen, got along as calmly and politely in England as it did.

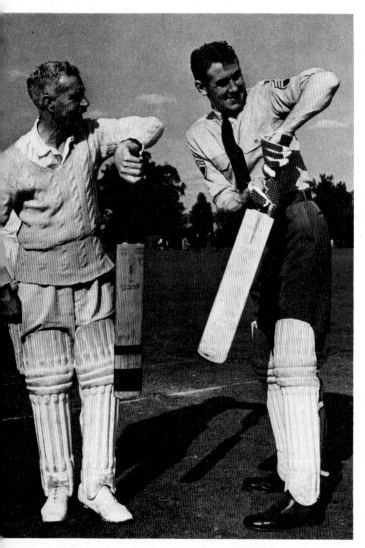

Army Sergeant and *Yank* photographer Slim Aarons gets a pointer on cricket batting from an instructor at Lord's, London's famed cricket ground. The picture appeared in a LIFE story on the War Department's *Short Guide to Great Britain*, a book of etiquette for U.S. servicemen.

The weekly Eighth Air Force softball game in London's Hyde Park gets underway in this painting by LIFE's artist-correspondent Floyd Davis.

◄ A chorus of 200 Air Force Engineers sings in London's Albert Hall in one of many good-will concerts given by this all-black outfit.

An American lights a London girl's cigarette, momentarily brightening the blackout in Picadilly Circus, headquarters for GIs on pass. The pole behind them is striped so that cars with blackout-dimmed lights will not strike it.

Americans count down to the longest day

General Eisenhower, Supreme Commander, eyes U.S. troops awaiting D-Day. Behind him is General Montgomery, head of the land forces.

Prime Minister Churchill inspects American paratroopers hardened for the invasion by repeated maneuvers in the U.S. and in Britain. ▼

With regimental colors flying and bayonets affixed to their rifles, GIs tramp in review across an English field. H-Hour was nearing for the long-planned Operation Overlord, the cross-Channel attack that was to be the greatest air-land-and-sea invasion in military history.

1944

New air power

Supreme Commander Ike

Wings over Asia

Far East bomber boss

Amphibious armor

Red Army chief

Fight for Iwo

General in Germany

Home-front artisan

1945

Pacific battlewagon

France's Grand Charles

Hollywood in uniform

Fleet Commander Nimitz

Destroyer power

The indomitable Winnie

V. FINALE

The Axis collapses in a thunderclap

Enter the Continent of Europe and undertake operations aimed at the heart of Germany and the destruction of her armed forces—orders to General Dwight D. Eisenhower, Supreme Commander, Allied Expeditionary Forces, February 12, 1944.

Despite the best plans ever laid for an amphibious invasion, Allied penetration of the Continent was a week-long hell of bloodshed and struggle against logistics, the elements and an army that had terrified the world. The Germans, like their Japanese partners whose home defenses were being breached on the other side of the world, fought more desperately as they were forced closer to their own soil. And mistakes were made. Because of the presumed need for surprise, the naval gunfire on Omaha Beach, the main U.S. objective at the base of the Cherbourg peninsula, was less than that budgeted for Tarawa (later acknowledged insufficient); the German defense installations on Omaha were three times as strong as those on Kwajalein, of recent bloody memory, and the defenders four times as many.

For a time the inclement weather that had delayed the landing lingered over Omaha. Landing craft were washed up sidewise onto the beach, and B-17s and B-24s, hampered by poor visibility, dropped many of their bombs on Norman apple orchards three miles inland. But the weather cleared, the mistakes were rectified and Hitler helped by making a bigger mistake. Considering the whole D-Day operation a diversion (British counterintelligence had spread word that the landing would be at Calais), he ordered no counterattack; the Navy guns moved in closer and the beachhead was secured.

In the Pacific, the casualties mounted fearsomely as the fighting neared Japan's home islands (of Japanese stubbornness LIFE's W. Eugene Smith commented, "When they fought that way we called it fanaticism; when we did, we called it bravery"). But progress never wavered, and B-29s springing from the reddened volcanic soil of Iwo Jima and Okinawa fire-bombed Japan's cities, starting with Tokyo. In Europe, the Berlin-bound Allies—and the folks on the U.S. home front, who thought the war was over—were rocked by the Germans' desperate counterattacks in the winter of 1944 and in early 1945 in the Ardennes and near Colmar in the Vosges. Clerks, typists and mess attendants were suddenly sent into combat. LIFE revealed that on some fronts U.S. troops were using 1918 ammunition. Warmer weather and reinforcements of armor revived the eastward push into Germany's heart. In Italy the Fifth Army broke through Kesselring's *Alpenjaeger* in the heavily mined Apennines and raced through the Po Valley to the Alpine wall guarding Austria. The Russians stormed through Poland and Finland in the north and Rumania and Bulgaria in the south, and entered Berlin on April 23. Hitler married Eva Braun, fired Göring and Himmler, and killed himself.

In the U.S., the waves of liberation were followed with joyous fascination, although the liberation of Paris was shadowed by the news of the Barnum and Bailey circus-tent fire at Hartford, Connecticut, which killed 162. Shirley Temple had married, and Hollywood discovered Elizabeth Taylor, 13, and Natalie Wood, 6. A useful new laboratory animal called a hamster was being imported from Syria, and a baffling new animal called a teenager was being discovered at home.

U.S. tourism flourished despite travel restrictions, and New York's subterranean Copacabana nightclub was jammed with visitors to the big city. In a special, issue-long "Letter to GIs," however, LIFE reassured them that the country was not going to the dogs. It said that jazz musician Pee Wee Russell was still going strong and that there was "no dearth of swing" or big bands; that many in war-booming New York "are in uniform like yourselves"; that the St. Louis Browns were the team to watch (for a while, anyway); that "you'll find your home block a little shabbier than you remember"; that "you can still buy a hot dog of sorts for a nickel"; and that Orphan Annie's Daddy Warbucks had died, "grieving over the decline of capitalism."

Harry Truman succeeded Franklin Roosevelt, who was mourned at his death as a war hero. At Potsdam, Truman relayed to Stalin the news of the A-bomb test blast at Los Alamos; Stalin shrugged. The Allies' unconditional-surrender demand was rejected by Japan, and Hiroshima replaced Armageddon as everyman's synonym for the apocalypse; the mushroom cloud became an instant symbol of the times. The last week of the war was the first week of the Atomic Age.

1944-1945

Overlord director Ike

D-Day: the Begining of the End

At 30 minutes past midnight on Tuesday, June 6, precisely six hours before H-Hour for the land attack, the first parachutists hit the silk over Normandy. At that moment, the U.S., British and Canadian armies of Operation Overlord had thousands of men afloat. The infantry, thankful at least that the suspense and false starts were over, plunged into the boiling surf at their appointed time. By 7:30 two American regiments and some tanks had made their way through breakers, shallow-water obstacles and German gunfire to the shore at "Utah" beach, the more westerly of two U.S. beachheads near the base of the Cherbourg peninsula (the other beach was "Omaha").

British forces headed for a beachhead some 20 miles farther east. There the waves were still choppy from bad weather on Sunday, and the German guns were more effectively zeroed in. As at the Americans' Omaha beach to the west, tanks were swamped and boats had a hard time unloading. But Allied warships and bombers rocked enemy gun emplacements and strong points all along the beach. By the week's end both western and eastern beaches were consolidated and the Allies were moving inland.

Beachhead veteran

First Army troops wade ashore on D-Day.

'I see my old mother'

Robert Capa sent this brief account of his D-Day landing experiences to LIFE:

I was going to Normandy on this nice, clean transport ship with a unit of the First Division. The food was good and we played poker. Once I filled an inside straight but I had four nines against me. Then just before 6 o'clock we were lowered in our LCVP and we started for the beach. It was rough and some of the boys were politely puking into paper bags. I always said this was a civilized invasion. We heard something popping around our boat but nobody paid any attention. We got out of the boat and started wading and then I saw men falling and had to push past their bodies. I said to myself, "This is not so good." I hid behind some tanks that were firing on the beach. After 20 minutes I suddenly realized that the tanks were what the Germans were shooting at 'so I made for the beach. I fell down next to a guy who looked at me and said, "You know what I see up there? I see my old mother sitting on the porch waving my insurance policy at me."

238

Robert Capa photographed men taking cover behind landing obstacles as they waited for a break in the firing, and then *(below)* edging toward the beach.

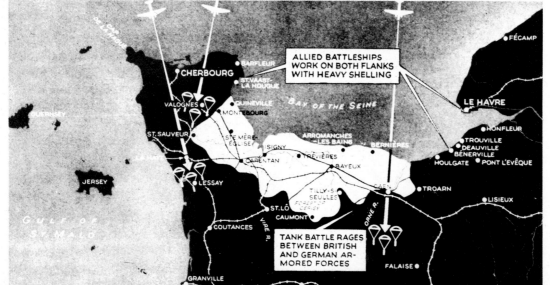

Omaha Beach a week after D-Day bustles with newly unloaded men and machines. Bad weather and heavy resistance hampered early phases of the landings.

A LIFE map traced the battle lines in Normandy 11 days after the invasion; Allied territory is shown in white. Planes from England had dropped paratroops, but the aircraft and their routes (arrows) are placed inaccurately, as are the parachutes indicating drop sites.

Reversing the pattern of Dunkirk, German POWs wade out to boats from which Americans had earlier waded in.

Standing on the soil of Normandy a few days after the first landings, Lieutenant General Omar N. Bradley, commander of the U.S. First Army, checks the disposition of Allied troops with high-ranking aides. "I don't see how the enemy can kick us out," Bradley said.

On June 12, the invasion's sixth day, the U.S. Chief of Staff, General George C. Marshall, washes up in a Normandy orchard. The four stars gleaming over the back of the GI helping him belong to General Henry H. "Hap" Arnold, commander of the Army Air Forces.

Artists view the breakthrough at St. Lô and Caen

In Bohrod's view of broken Caen, where the fighting lasted longest and the damage was the worst, British and Canadian infantrymen move

An MP directs traffic before a cross festooned with Signal Corps wires in Aaron Bohrod's painting of action in France after the defeat of beach defenses. This village, Pont-l'Abbé, won with help from the French underground, was less badly damaged than in 17th Century religious wars.

past civilians trying to resume their lives. A cart carries flower-decked coffins. For 11 days Germans in the suburbs shelled the city's center. ▼

Ogden M. Pleissner painted Normans in a coastal town *(bottom, left)* waving to a 3,000-plane armada headed for the St. Lô front on June

25. After the breakthrough, he painted German troops *(below)* surrendering to U.S. Sherman tanks, which poured through St. Lô.

The twice-lived war of Private Teed: LIFE takes a veteran on a sentimental journey

In a nostalgic mood as the magazine neared its 25th anniversary in 1960, LIFE's editors were inspired to look up an old friend. When they had last seen Charles Teed, he was a 22-year-old draftee from Effingham, Illinois, training at Fort Bragg, North Carolina, and they had put him on the cover. After marrying his childhood sweetheart, he shipped out in 1942 with the Ninth Infantry for Casablanca, Sicily, Utah Beach and St. Lô. There bullets shattered his left arm, tore open a lung and sent him home after two years in the hospital.

Improbably, LIFE found civilian Teed, 41, right back in Effingham, running a TV repair business. The magazine sent Teed with photographer Leonard McCombe on a memory-haunted reenactment of his past, from Fort Bragg to Normandy. It published in its Silver Jubilee issue "the life of Charles Teed, a companion with whom LIFE is proud to have shared the era."

"I remember the hedgerows in Normandy," said Teed *(right)*, reenacting his experiences in 1960 with U.S. soldiers. "A dirty place to fight."

Teed gazes grimly from a Sicilian mountain. "They used to bring our food and supplies up on mules and sometimes even they would fall." ▼

Pilgrim Teed stands lost in thought in the American Cemetery at Omaha Beach. He had looked up the locations of the crosses and stars that mark the graves of the men who had fought beside him. Teed landed in Normany on D-plus-4, and before being wounded, he had begun to believe that he was overdue to die. "You never can picture yourself getting it," he told McCombe. "But I'd been out a long time and it figured."

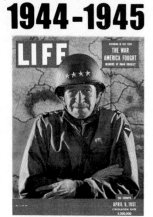

Bradley in triumph

Invader from the south

Surrender in France

The Americans had St. Lô and the British had Caen, but the fighting south of those hard-won points settled down to a costly, hedgerow-to-hedgerow crawl. To push the Germans out of Normandy, Lieutenant General Bradley devised a plan, called Cobra, to use bombers to clear the way for ground troops. He laid out a rectangular carpet, three and a half miles broad by one and a half miles deep, for saturation bombing.

On July 25, after a false start in which a few planes dropped bombs on Major General Lawton Collins' VII Corps, more than 2,400 Allied bombers dropped 4,000 tons on the carpet. The infantry, although still close enough to be hit again by "friendly" bombs, advanced. The Americans had reached Avranches by August 1, and Lieutenant General Patton's Third Army tanks, in a spreading, three-pronged, free-wheeling attack, burst into Brittany. They swung left to cut off the German Seventh Army, which was being frontally attacked by the U.S. First Army. General Montgomery at the same time pressed south from Caen and took Falaise, and his Canadians almost joined up with Patton at Argentan. Enough of a gap was left for Field Marshal Günther von Kluge to extricate some 30,000 men, but 10,000 were killed and 50,000 were captured. Meanwhile, U.S. troops under Lieutenant General Lucian K. Truscott were landing in the south near Marseilles. The Germans, nearly finished in France, salvaged what they could and headed east.

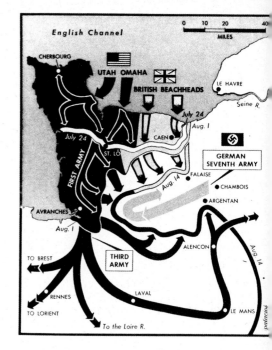

Below St. Lô, the Americans swept into Brittany and outflanked the Germans, who were trapped between the U.S. and British.

A German prisoner in Normandy, his war over and a strip of wool on his lip, burlesques his erstwhile supreme commander, Adolf Hitler.

At a field conference with General Bradley, General Montgomery, Allied ground forces commander, eyes Third Army chief Patton's sidearm.

A liberated people rejoice

That France was being returned to the French sent what LIFE called a "shock of elation" through the civilized world. In France that elation was written on every face, and wherever Allied soldiers walked or rode they were met with smiles, cheers and flowers. Photographers snapped GIs kissing mademoiselles in every liberated hamlet. No one received a more impassioned welcome than Charles de Gaulle, who eight days after the Normandy landing was on French soil for the first time since 1940, and setting up his government.

It was Paris, of course, that the world watched come back to life. Parisians crowded the Cafe de la Paix drinking *demi-blondes*, and the kiosks across the street sold maps of Paris and postcards with De Gaulle's picture. Reporters looked to their favorite landmarks for signs of damage—the Hotel Crillon looked beaten-up, but Notre Dame showed only machine-gun pock marks that would merge with the scars of time. Correspondent Charles Wertenbaker found that some good had come out of the occupation. French girls between 18 and 21, Wertenbaker reported, were "more beautiful than French girls ever were before. They walked and bicycled as they grew up and did not eat too much."

Little girls behind a hedgerow of flowers wait for Charles de Gaulle in Isigny, only days after the Allies freed it. The crowd had only 20 minutes' notice of the General's arrival. His assumption of governmental powers was not fully accepted by the Allies, who wanted more of France liberated before he took over. But playwright Henri Bernstein said: "This is not going to make him unpopular among the French."

Police and air-raid wardens restrain Parisians trying to see De Gaulle. Correspondents expected the happiness but not the healthiness of the people. Paris had been on short rations, but because much of its food came from Normandy, its worst shortages came after D-Day. ▲

On the hood of a half-track, a soldier of the Seventh Army receives a typical liberator's reward from a young woman of Chartres.

In Ralph Morse's historic picture, ▶ Charles de Gaulle walks down the Champs Elysées with civilian resistance fighters following.

After liberation, the bar at the Hotel Scribe in Paris is jammed with a collection of journalists and pundits painted by LIFE artist Floyd Davis (seated at left with his wife Gladys). Standing next to Davis is *March of Time* producer Richard de Rochemont, and next to Gladys Davis, with camera, is LIFE photographer David Scherman. LIFE correspondent Will Lang stares gravely ahead at center. *Time* Paris bureau chief Charles

Wertenbaker chats under De Gaulle's portrait, and LIFE photographer Ralph Morse holds a Nazi flag. Behind his hands loom LIFE photographer Robert Capa and pipe-smoking writer Noel Busch. Seated at the center table are eye-patched broadcaster William Shirer, Ernest Hemingway and *The New Yorker*'s Janet Flanner. Commentator H. V. Kaltenborn stands (with arms behind back) at extreme right.

A man suspected of having collaborated with German occupiers tries to shield his face from a Breton's blow in Bob Landry's classic picture.

Ex-Premier Edouard Herriot shouts, "J'accuse!" at the treason trial of Marshal Henri Pétain, the aging president of Vichy France. ▼

old scores with their collaborating countrymen

In Robert Capa's famous photograph of French vigilante justice, jeering citizens of Chartres haze a woman whose head has been shaved because her baby was fathered by a German. Seized with vindictive frenzy after the Liberation, Frenchmen denounced and jailed collaborators.

LIFE reports in pictures

Three California girls celebrate D-Day, June 6, 1944, on the beach, their complexions protected by newspapers bearing banner headlines of the landing in northern France. D-Day was the biggest news since Pearl Harbor, and crowds snapped up every paper on sale.

Ballyhoo for Thomas E. Dewey at the Chicago G.O.P. convention included a troop of models who posed with bigshots and handed out buttons.

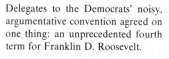

A New York heat wave and the ready money of full employment draw crowds to Brooklyn's Coney Island. Public beaches like this one and elegant private resorts were full of vacationers, who jammed trains running to the seashore despite the continued restrictions on civilian travel.

Delegates to the Democrats' noisy, argumentative convention agreed on one thing: an unprecedented fourth term for Franklin D. Roosevelt.

Just home from the hospital after having a baby—Harry James was the father—Betty Grable plays ball at poolside with the family poodle.

A sign in a gas station proclaims a fuel drought. When available, gas was limited to a gallon and a half per week for ordinary motorists.

A more cheerful notice nestles among bottles at a liquor store. Booze, recently sold only by the bottle, could now be bought in cases.

what happened here between D-Day and the attack on Germany

Workmen eye a locomotive derailed near McKees Rocks, Pennyslvania. Increasing age and overuse of rolling stock caused more frequent wrecks.

Two U.S. deputy marshals grab a black marketeer who has knocked down a photographer attempting to take his picture.

Cary Grant and Barbara Hutton, shown in a LIFE 1942 wedding picture, separated but shared a house because of the housing shortage.

Used with the permission of the Publisher, Williamson Music, Inc.

Top pop song in the summer of 1944, "I'll Be Seeing You," came out in 1938, but became a hit as more and more people missed one another.

The most popular stage musical was *Oklahoma!* It opened March 31, 1943, and in a year and a half had been seen by more than 960,000 people.

Barry Fitzgerald gives new assistant Bing Crosby advice based on years of experience as a parish priest in the sentimental hit film, *Going My Way*.

This flier reminded shoppers that some goods were still buyable only with blue stamps, but low-grade beef was unrationed by 1944.

While training in a Florida foxhole, Private Charles E. Lee learns that he is a father of quadruplets and grins— but remains seated.

Democratic candidates Truman and Roosevelt confer on the White House lawn. F. D. R.'s lined face and dark-circled eyes showed his fatigue.

Eight-inch ammo eater

The Assault on Germany: First Phase

After their Normandy victory, the Allies raced eastward, speedily liberating not only northern France but also most of Belgium, Luxembourg and that part of Holland not bristling with defenses for the launch sites of Hitler's V-weapons *(pages 262–263)*. People at home began to get the feeling, incorrectly it developed, that the war was practically over.

For the troops, the picture changed abruptly at the German border. There were no liberated townspeople welcoming them and helping to seize bridges and round up prisoners. There were only German soldiers defending their homeland, who

were aided in that by the overextension of Allied supply lines.

The First Army battled its way through the Hürtgen Forest in the border region—10 weeks of fighting in the shadow of tall firs—up to the Roer River. As winter approached, the fighting along the 450-mile front was a struggle in which progress came to be measured in yards. Covering the last 25 miles to Cologne and the Ruhr, the First Army, with the U.S. Ninth and the British Second, moved against a foe who fought ferociously for every house and trench. It was a test of strength reminiscent of the Meuse-Argonne fighting of World War I.

The advance in the gloomy Hürtgen Forest was foot by foot

In September 1944 U.S. troops entered the Hürtgen Forest, 50 gloomy square miles of firs and German pillboxes. Two and a half murderous months later they emerged exhausted and hungry, only to have their victory threatened by the Bulge (page 264). Following is a part of William Walton's cable to LIFE:

The Twelfth Regiment, under hoarse-voiced Colonel Bob Chance, worked foot by foot up a forested slope with two companies driving a wedge into the German lines, a wedge that threatened the German positions but also exposed the two companies' flanks. The German mortars, wise to the terrain, cracked into F and G Companies, bursting in the trees to shower jagged fragments for yards around. Machine guns ripped the gloom and rifles crackled as the Germans gave a little ground, but only a little.

Seeing the two companies worm into their lines, the Germans waited. Then they threw in mortar fire and under its protection struck down a ravine and up the other side to cut the slim supply line. F and G Companies were trapped.

For two days and nights the Germans poured mortar and artillery shells into the narrow area where infantrymen back to back were fighting off the German attacks. One slender footpath brought a trickle of ammunition but no food or water. The path was under such constant fire that the wounded could not be evacuated. Rain drizzled through the darkness, trickling into foxholes and seeping through winter clothing. Medical supplies were insufficient to care for men with jagged leg wounds, with bleeding chests, missing fingers, blood- and rain-soaked bandages.

E Company, nearest to their surrounded comrades, tried desperately to relieve them. On the third day Colonel Chance moved up A and C Companies in the darkness and sent them in to attack at daylight. The Germans, caught between the isolated companies and their relief, were slaughtered. On both sides there was slaughter, but F and G Companies had been saved. That was how every foot of the Hürtgen Forest was to be. Then it snowed. The roads, already brown rivulets, remained quagmires that sucked down tanks, trucks and jeeps struggling to the front.

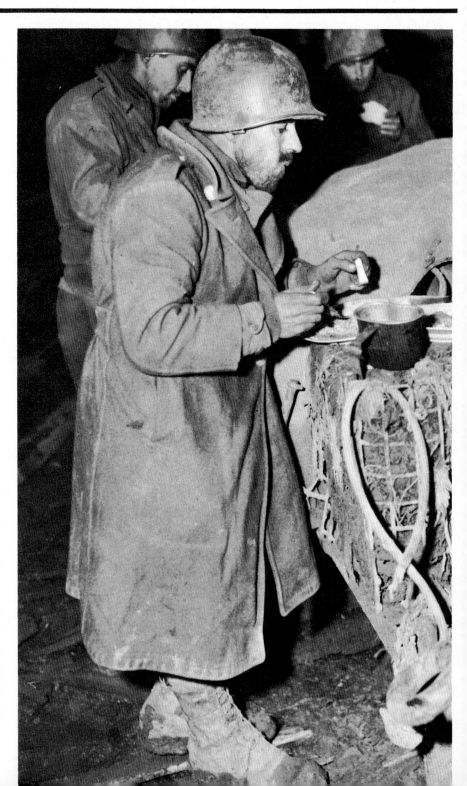

◀ Bone-weary Americans who fought in one of the Hürtgen Forest battles eat their first hot meal in 15 days. At times the fighting was so severe that replacements that were trucked up to the front would suffer more than 50 per cent casualties before they even got into the line.

An overturned German tank, its belly smeared with the mud of the western front's incessant fall rains, is inspected by U.S. soldiers. The tank had toppled into a crater after an Allied plane dropped a heavy bomb squarely in front of it. Everyone in its crew was dead.

The British take a Dutch canal

Battling painfully across canal- and river-laced southeast Holland, Scottish troops slog through mud and smoke toward the Wessem Canal.

Infantrymen, accompanied by LIFE photographer George Silk, push off toward the enemy shore, which is ablaze from tank flame throwers. ▼

Across the canal, despite heavy mortar and machine-gun fire, a British gunner fires at Germans beyond a line of burning haystacks.

Germans emerge from smoke- and flame-swept dugouts to surrender. The Tommies' next objective: the next canal. ▼

1944-1945

Lott back home

Medical Odyssey of a Wounded GI

The time: 11:30 a.m., November 22, 1944. The place: a battlefield in Lorraine. A Third Army medic named George Lott scrambled out of a creekbed to answer the cries of a wounded man—and was instantly hit in both arms by fragments of an exploding German mortar shell. "Gee, doc, I feel like both my arms were blown off," Lott told a surgeon after staggering 500 yards back to the battalion aid station. There to record that moment (below, top left) was Ralph Morse, who would begin a 4,500-mile, 30-day odyssey. He followed Lott by foot, train and plane through two more dressing stations, and five hospitals in France, England and the U.S.

Morse's tour de force provided LIFE readers with a cover and 13 pages of pictures. They showed step by step the kind of Army Medical Corps treatment that saved more than 96 per cent of those wounded in combat who reached hospitals. Not just a case of frontline luck, the report had been meticulously planned. Long before meeting Lott, Morse had cabled for permission to show the remarkable medical treatment he had seen GIs receiving since Guadalcanal. He got approval from the Surgeon General to follow a wounded man wherever the treatment might take him. For weeks, after the story of the agonizing journey appeared, Lott was inundated with money, hundreds of pounds of candy, cookies, fruit, jam, nuts, olives, cigars and cigarettes. He also received thousands of letters thanking him "and all the other GIs" for bravery. With one arm amputated, he is living today in Albany, New York.

Minutes after being wounded, a stunned Lott is helped by medics.

Less than an hour later, Lott smokes while getting a morphine shot.

Soldiers carry Lott from an ambulance to a casualty collecting station.

Surgeons at base hospital write information on the unconscious Lott's cast.

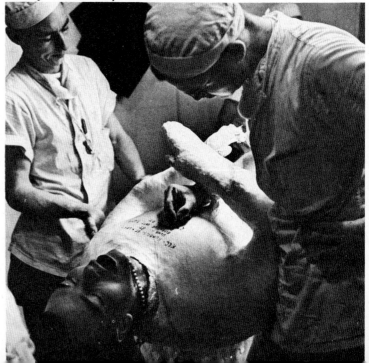

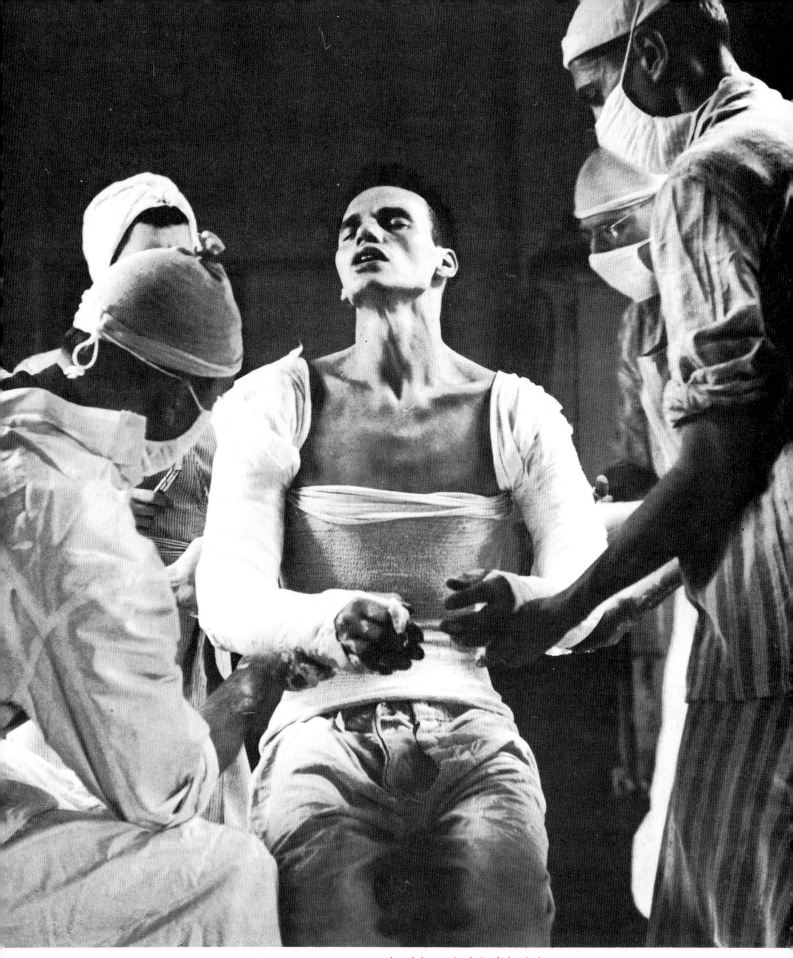

Lott grimaces in pain as Army doctors in a British hospital mold a new plaster cast to his body. Lott's right arm was so badly shattered that although he regained circulation in it for a time, it was eventually amputated at his own request in the Battle Creek, Michigan, V.A. hospital.

V for Vengeance

Vengeance weapons *(Vergeltungswaffen)* aimed at Britain and an explosive counteroffensive on the western front *(overleaf)* were last-ditch German efforts to regain the initiative between 1944 and 1945. The new weapons were launched from sites until these bases were captured by the Allies. The earliest weapons were pilotless aircraft that the British called V-1s, or buzz bombs. They were stuffed with explosives and powered by noisy jet engines that shut off over England, where they fell at random. Even more terrifying were the later V-2 rockets, progenitors of today's ballistic missiles, which flew so fast—3,600 miles per hour—they arrived without warning.

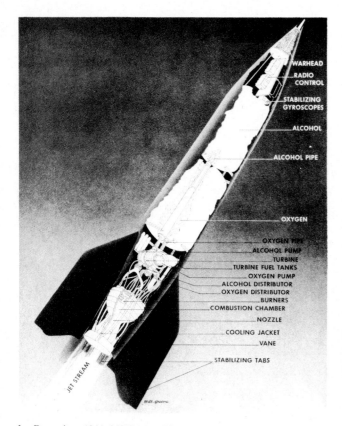

In December 1944 LIFE ran this drawing of a V-2 rocket, which is accurate from the gyroscopic guidance system to the powerful engine.

Over the North Sea a Heinkel 111 bomber releases a pilotless V-1. They were deployed from planes after launching sites were captured.

London children, forced by V-1s to evacuate the city once again, prepare to board a train for transportation to the countryside.

Helmeted rescue workers move through the dust of a V-1 explosion that wrecked a bus and wounded the woman they are carrying.

PATTON

LIFE

JANUARY 15, 1945 10 CENTS
YEARLY SUBSCRIPTION $4.50

Reinforcer of Bastogne

The Bulge: Hitler's Last Effort

It was supposed to be a quiet sector—a good place to be during the week before Christmas 1944. The men of the U.S. Fourth Division, relieved from the hellish Hürtgen Forest fighting *(pages 256-257),* were cleaning their weapons and relaxing with some local Luxembourg beer. The weather was terrible and Army Air Forces' operations were limited. Then, on December 16, the enemy's usually sporadic artillery stepped up. Hitler was about to launch a counterattack that would take the Allies completely by surprise. His plan was to drive north across Belgium to Antwerp—via Liége and Bastogne in the Ardennes—and cut the Allied front in two. As the attack went on, the thinly held center gave way, and a bulge swelled toward the Meuse River.

At Bastogne, Brigadier General Anthony C. McAuliffe and his 101st Airborne were cut off. When emissaries of General Hasso von Manteuffel demanded that McAuliffe surrender, he got a classically laconic answer: "Nuts!" Within days, Lieutenant General Patton's Fourth Armored Division was fighting for the relief of the Bulge along with other Allied units. Flying weather improved and the threat ended.

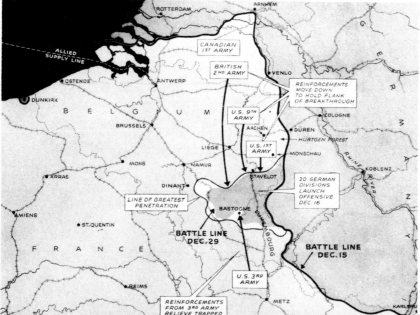

In this German photograph, dead Americans are stripped of equipment by scavenging Nazis in the Ardennes. One man was robbed of his shoes.

The Bulge disrupted the Allied timetable. Three German armies diverted four Allied armies from Ruhr and Saar drives.

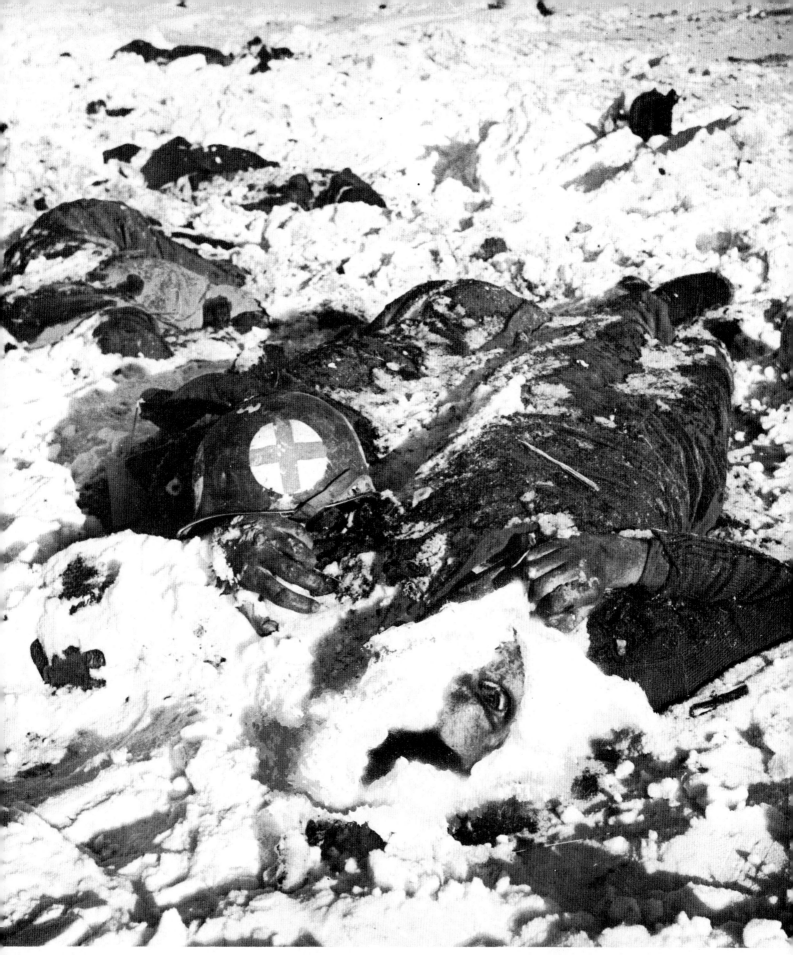

The most frightful by-product of the Battle of the Bulge occurred on the second day of the breakthrough. Near Malmédy, German tanks over-powered a column of American trucks. A Nazi officer ordered 159 Americans herded into a field where most were cut down with a Schmeisser machine pistol at point-blank range. Those who remained alive were shot in the head. But 15 men who had run into a wood survived. Weeping with rage, they returned to tell of the massacre. John Florea's picture of a murdered medic was retouched to obscure his face.

Winter-front infantryman

Assault on Germany: Final Phase

Once the Bulge was flattened, Allied armies knifed through the Siegfried Line, burst across the Rhine and laced Germany with columns whose progress on war maps looked like the lines on the palm of a hand. The progress of the Ninth Army in the north depended on the prior capture, by the First Army, of the dams that controlled the level of the meandering Roer River west of the Rhine. The crossing of the Rhine itself was effected by quick, low-level parachute drops on the east bank and the seizure of the bridge at Remagen. The First Army would link up with the advancing Russians east of Leipzig in late April.

The Roer dam operation and the bold parachute drops across the Rhine opened Germany to the final assault. Churchill visiting the Rhine front cried, "The German is whipped; we've got him; he is all through." As rhetorical utterances go, the P.M.'s was essentially accurate on strategic grounds. But it might have rung hollow to the men doing the actual fighting for the next six weeks. Two actions in particular provided LIFE photographers with opportunities to picture two kinds of modern combat from unusually close quarters. Robert Capa, making the chute drop east of the Rhine, recorded a daring and risky airborne operation (pages 268-269). Accompanying the troops on the Roer crossing, George Silk became involved in the bloody, small-scale operation shown on these pages.

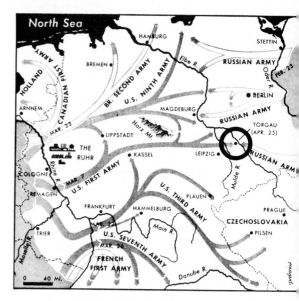

After the Bulge, the First and Ninth armies strike east as the British swing north. The circle marks the first meeting with the Russians.

On the Roer's east bank, U.S. engineers, with whom Silk crossed on their pontoon bridge, edge toward German snipers on the bridge.

Some of the Germans walk out holding their handkerchiefs as white flags. Others, who fired a number of ▼ shots at the engineers, were killed.

Two engineers herd the prisoners back to the bridge. Just after Silk took this picture, one of the PWs dropped a live hand grenade.

The grenade thrower lies dead (right). One engineer was wounded and another was killed. Silk was hit ▼ in the leg and flown back to England.

On the footbridge, one of several the engineers erected, the body of a GI lies where he was hit by mortar-shell fragments, just 50 feet short of the east bank. The crossing had been attempted a month earlier, but the Germans opened the upper Roer dam gates. This flooded the lower valley and forced Ninth Army commander General William H. Simpson to postpone the operation until the gates had been captured.

Tanks drive to the Rhine and chutists overleap it

In a textbook illustration on the art of tank warfare (taken from a light spotter plane by George Silk), Ninth Army tanks imprint Rhine Valley farmland near Cologne with a map of their deployment. The houses beyond the tanks have been set afire by U.S. dive bombers and artillery. Behind the houses, German self-propelled guns have opened fire on the tanks. The armor had been running along the road in the foreground and had fanned out in attack formation to deal with the self-propelled guns. The Rhine is visible a little over two miles away. On the opposite page are Robert Capa's pictures of a different kind of Rhine attack near the Dutch border 50 miles to the northwest. Capa parachuted into Germany with the U.S. Seventeenth Airborne Division and the British Sixth Airborne Division.

U.S. paratroopers attacking near Wesel are joined by British glider-borne infantrymen as they race toward houses under German fire.

After clearing Germans from their landing area, the paratroopers move out across the fields. In the foreground a machine gunner sets up.

A German mother and her children, evicted (with a precious pair of shoes) by the fighting, occupy a foxhole vacated by advancing paratroopers.

◄ A medical corpsman treats a soldier hit in the early fighting. Other medics in the drop immediately started setting up an aid station.

Underneath a parachute draped over telephone wires, a paratrooper carries a wounded buddy, with full kit, to a first-aid station.

Roosevelt's favorite picture, taken in 1939, shows the "zestful amateur" sailor-President watching fleet maneuvers aboard the U.S.S. *Houston*.

In Tom McAvoy's candid picture, F. D. R.'s omnipresent cigarette holder tilts jauntily at a Jefferson-▼Jackson Day dinner in Washington.

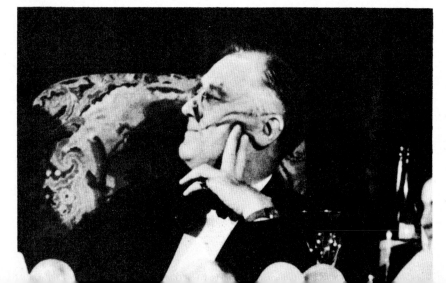

Death of a Leader

On April 12, 1945, in a frame cottage on Pine Mountain, Georgia, Franklin Delano Roosevelt died of a massive cerebral hemorrhage. Around the globe—on beleaguered Okinawa in the Pacific, in the mountains of northern Italy and the rubbled cities of the Ruhr—Americans were struck with sorrow and momentarily stopped whatever they were doing. LIFE's editors, who had often been critical of F. D. R., wrote: "Americans will not soon forget the jut of his chin, the angle of his cigarette holder, his smile. This gallant, fearless man, who could not stand on his own feet without help, bestrode his country like a giant through great and changeful years. His death had an immediate impact on the world that the death of no other American has ever had. He died with victory for all he believed in at last in sight."

Two months before his death, Roosevelt meets with Churchill and Stalin at Yalta, where postwar Europe was carved up by the Big Three.

LIFE's Ed Clark caught the nation's sorrow in the face of this Navy musician as F. D. R.'s body was carried from his Warm Springs cottage. ▼

◄ F. D. R. and King George VI chat amiably as they ride through Washington in 1939, the year British monarchs visited the U.S. for the first time.

Looking wan and thin after being elected to a fourth term in 1944, Roosevelt waves to supporters while Mrs. Roosevelt stands by solicitously.

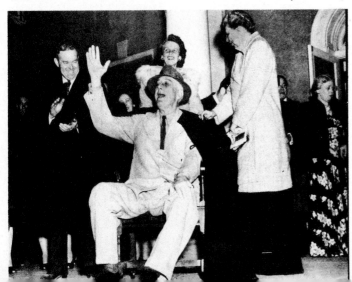

Linkup with Ivan on the Elbe

The progress of the Western Allies, driving almost unhindered across Germany, finally matched that of the Russians sweeping all before them in the east. On April 25 they met on the Elbe River at the town of Torgau. The exact zones that each side were to occupy thereafter had been carefully worked out by Allied government heads two months before. But this high-level arrangement aroused the disgust of Allied generals eager to sweep eastward to Berlin and frustrated westward-fleeing Germans desperate to surrender to the British or Americans rather than to the vengeful Russians.

For the Red Army, the advance to Berlin was the culmination of a German retreat that made Napoleon's evacuation of Russia 133 years earlier look like a romp in the snow. For the Wehrmacht, it was a bitter, backward-slogging fire fight of 2,000 miles. The final battles virtually leveled Berlin and added eastern Germany to the list of European carnage.

LIFE had followed the Red Army's course with frank admiration, remarking at one point that it "was carrying most of the fighting load in Europe." The cost was high. America lost 155,000 men. Eight million Russian soldiers died.

In a spectacular celebration of yet another Soviet victory, fireworks explode in the dark above Moscow's Red Square. Such displays, ordered by Stalin, were held with increasing frequency in 1944 as city after city fell to the Red Army.

◀ A squad of cheerful Russian tommy gunners relaxes in a field in front of a Mark IV tank that they captured on their way to Germany.

Grimy but happy American and Russian lieutenants embrace near the little Elbe River town of Torgau, some 75 miles from Hitler's capital.

1944-1945

A GI "heils" Hitler

Surrender en Masse

With peace only hours away, GIs still die. As Robert Capa was

Germany surrendered at 2:41 a.m. on Monday, May 7, 1945. That was the minute when German armed forces chief General Alfred Jodl, at a plain wood table in a grimy school building in Reims, signed the paper that ended 2,076 days of war in Europe. But the Germans had been surrendering in various parts of the Continent for days. They surrendered piecemeal—first by the thousands as disorganized regiments and divisions gave up, then by the hundreds of thousands as the armies in Italy and Austria laid down their arms.

Before giving up his forces in north Germany to Field Marshal Montgomery, Admiral Hans von Friedeburg, the most recent commander of the German Navy, tried to split the Allies by offering to turn over three German armies that had been fighting the Russians. Monty refused. Von Friedeburg capitulated, but the next day, reporting to Eisenhower in Reims in an attempt to surrender all of Germany's forces, he made a similar offer, saying he was empowered to deal with the Western Allies but not with the Russians. The Supreme Commander turned him down too, and it was not until Jodl arrived that the signing could take place.

With the final surrender signature, the Allies' prime task became the guarding and feeding of the millions of prisoners. For Ike it was the happiest of problems. "This," he said proudly, "is a battlefield surrender."

General Eisenhower flaunts surrender pens. With him are Lieutenant General Walter Bedell Smith, Ike's secretary Kay Summersby and his deputy Sir Arthur Tedder.

◄ The end comes in north Germany as Admiral Hans von Friedeburg (facing camera) surrenders 600,000 men to Field Marshal Montgomery.

Some 160,000 German prisoners set up a pup tent stockade on a German plain. They were a fraction of the four million who surrendered.

photographing two of them on a balcony in Leipzig (their faces blocked out by the censor) one was killed by a German sniper across the way.

Legacy of Horror

The final onslaught on Germany by Allied forces in the early spring of 1945 uncovered its infamous concentration camps. Battle-hardened troops were horrified by scenes of inhumanity that ordinary Germans either chose to ignore or had become inured to.

Dachau, Bergen-Belsen, Buchenwald, Theresienstadt. The names became stigmatic synonyms for a horror that was indeed incredible—the deliberate mass murder of millions of men, women and children as the Nazis zealously implemented Adolf Hitler's "Final Solution."

Emaciated corpses stacked like cordwood, gas chambers and crematoria, where thousands of human beings a day were "processed," reflected a ghastly mockery of efficiency that reached its nadir in a Polish concentration camp called Auschwitz. There all that remained of some four million prisoners were mounds of spectacles, baby shoes and human hair. In all, some six million Jews were murdered, in addition to unnumbered thousands of political prisoners, mental patients, gypsies and others who failed to qualify as racially pure by the definitions that Hitler had ordained.

In a Buchenwald barracks, emaciated prisoners freed by the Allies grin feebly and sip U.S. rations. Those on the lower bunk are too weak to eat.

A boy walks past corpses at Bergen-Belsen. GIs could not comprehend the Germans' unconcern with the existence of the death camps.   ▼

The living dead stare out at their Allied rescuers in Margaret Bourke-White's grim photograph of Buchenwald prisoners. Those who were able to stand sometimes survived, but many others did not. At Bergen-Belsen it was reported that 300 of the liberated inmates died every day.

The tables turned, an SS officer and a female guard stand knee deep in bodies. They were given the chore of burying their victims.

This young prisoner tried to squeeze ▶ under a door in an attempt to escape a building set afire by the Nazis as American soldiers approached.

1944-1945

Backwash of the Debacle

Adolf Hitler's Thousand Year Reich ended 988 years prematurely in the spring of 1945. The Führer himself was dead, by his own hand in a Berlin bunker with Eva Braun, his wife of only a day and a half. It was an act that was echoed by suicides among defeated Nazis high and low. Top-level officials who could be found and arrested were held for a war crimes tribunal. Hitler's ally Mussolini had met an ignominious end when he and his mistress were caught and executed by Italian *partigiani (opposite)*.

Throughout Germany, wrote correspondent Sidney Olson, there moved "the most motley crowds that Europe has seen since the Crusades." There were homeless Poles, Czechs, Hungarians and Russians, and then suddenly millions of homeless Germans. A new nation of DPs (displaced persons) scrounged for shelter and food.

In the ranks of those they had made homeless, there was scant compassion for the German DPs. Whenever Allied troops were not looking, they took revenge on their former tormentors by pillaging the cities and towns once hailed as foundations of the New Order.

Arriving at a Berlin station pocked with Russian rocket holes, civilians and soldiers swell the population by eight million in the month following Germany's surrender.

In Schweinfurt a neighbor covers two children of a Nazi. Their widowed mother had bandaged their eyes, killed them, then shot herself.

Exhausted refugees *(above)* huddle in a Berlin building. At left, a young DP rests with her belongings and dog in the ruins of Cologne.

A toppled tyrant and his mistress hang in death

In 1947 Laszlo Bush-Fekete, a Hungarian playwright, visited Mezzegra near Como, Italy, and reconstructed the end of Benito Mussolini and Claretta Petacci, his mistress. The playwright's account of Il Duce's capture by partisans while trying to escape to Switzerland ends as follows:

Claretta and Mussolini, side by side, squeezed tightly against the wall.

At that moment Valerio (who had pretended to be Mussolini's rescuer) stepped back three paces and began to speak.

"I hereby carry out the verdict of the tribunal of the people of Italy." And he pointed his Tommy gun at Mussolini. Claretta threw herself in front of Mussolini.

"No! No! He mustn't die!" she screamed.

"Get away from there or you'll die with him," Valerio shouted. Then he pulled the trigger, but the gun misfired. Thereupon he drew his revolver and took aim. The second weapon also misfired. Mussolini and Claretta stared at him numbly. The Duce clutched the edge of the stone wall. Valerio rushed over to one of the partisans, grabbed the Sten gun from his hands and turned back to the wall. Mussolini and Claretta watched all this, motionless.

The Sten gun worked. Five bullets struck Mussolini. He collapsed without uttering a sound. Claretta stood over him, still staring rigidly at Valerio. Four more bullets rattled from the gun. The Duce's mistress dropped to the ground. Mussolini had slumped down to a sitting position at the foot of the wall and, in falling, Claretta's body nudged him so that his head fell on her breast. Mussolini was still alive. Valerio stepped up to him and shot him twice, at point-blank range. A thin trickle of blood appeared at the corner of Mussolini's mouth and then dripped down his coat. Valerio started off in his car toward Milan to report that the verdict had been carried out.

1944–1945

Happy Homecomings

Home is the sailor

Four and a half million American fighting men in Europe greeted V-E Day as a reprieve, especially those who had seen months, if not years, of hazardous duty. Certainly they were proud to have beaten the Germans; but just as important, the victory meant that they could now get out of the service. Nobody was thinking much about readjusting to civilian life. And even the dreams—buying a car, a steak, a decent cup of coffee, or getting a chance to confront the First Sergeant in civvies—still seemed remote. For the moment, the big things were returning Stateside and getting out.

Getting out wasn't always easy. As the military bureaucracy struggled with the enormous task of demobilizing so many men, bottlenecks developed that frustrated the servicemen and delayed the process. Under the point system, men with the most points—based on the type of combat, length of service, age and state of health—were rotated home first. Those with the fewest points had occupation duty in Germany to look forward to. But in time all but a very small minority—mostly officers and those who were sent to the Pacific—came home to be called Mister once again.

◄Frontline cartoonist Bill Mauldin, whose dogfaces Willie and Joe *(pages 230–231)* honored the GI. cuddles his son Bruce for photographer Martha

Holmes. Bruce, who was born while Mauldin was in Sicily, is now an Army major, with two tours of duty as a helicopter pilot in Vietnam.

An even more famous soldier home on rotation, Dwight D. Eisenhower, claps Mayor Fiorello LaGuardia on the shoulder as they meet in New

York. In a triumphal ride through Manhattan, Ike was cheered by four million people, more than had turned out for Charles Lindbergh.

281

Returning soldiers cover every topside inch of the British superliner *Queen Mary* as she steams into New York harbor. The *Queen* had transported 650,000 soldiers without convoy to Europe, the Far East and the Pacific since March 1941. Now she was bringing a few of them home.

Warmest welcome home of all went to a lucky GI on the Second Division's troopship *Monticello.* He bent down just as Marlene Dietrich got a boost from three delighted soldiers holding onto her famous legs—and received one of the most dramatic hello kisses ever recorded on film. ▶

MacArthur victorious

Mac Returns—Twice

"I shall return," General MacArthur had told the Philippine people when he left Corregidor in a PT boat on the night of March 12, 1942. On October 20, 1944, two years, seven months and nine days later, he waded ashore *(right)* on Leyte island, making good the most celebrated promise in U.S. military history. Two months later, LIFE's Carl Mydans, who had been with MacArthur when Manila fell and had been taken prisoner—and later repatriated—also returned to the Philippines. Leyte had fallen after fierce resistance, and Mydans was just in time to catch MacArthur making his "return" official by repeating it *(below)* at Luzon.

The two returns renewed the binge of MacArthur worship that had started in 1942, when the General safely reached Australia from Corregidor, and did not end with victory in 1945 *(left)*. Throughout that period, in veneration of "the first great national hero of the age," as LIFE called him, Americans lavished his name on streets, dances (the MacArthur Glide), flowers (the MacArthur Camellia, the Mrs. MacArthur Sweet Pea), canal locks and babies. "In all the United Nations," said LIFE, "his name was magic."

A cartoon MacArthur was "The Colossus of the Pacific."

Landing on Leyte with the Sixth Army, General MacArthur sets historic foot on Philippine soil. Eighty days later *(far left)*, he makes his return again, striding through Lingayen Gulf waters to the shore of the Philippines' main island, Luzon.

By act of Congress, Washington's Conduit Road becomes MacArthur Boulevard. MacArthur was a favorite subject of Los Angeles Federal Art Project members, who painted for GIs *(opposite, right)*. One batch of requests for V.I.P. paintings ran: MacArthur 35, Lincoln and Washington six each, F. D. R. two.

The Marines meet something new: enemy civilians

As the island hoppers approached Japan, a new horror was added to their war: the suicidal resistance of civilians. Saipan, the 72-square mile Marianas island that two Marine divisions and one Army division had invaded even before the final capture of the Philippines, was Japanese home territory. Its 25,000 civilians were not Melanesians but predominantly Japanese, imbued with the national philosophy that suicide as "a shield for the Emperor" is the most honorable of deaths.

Their propaganda had told the civilians they would be killed if captured. Still, a modest number surrendered during the 25 days of battle. But others, like those pictured here by LIFE's W. Eugene Smith, were found in caves with uniformed defenders, who had to be blasted out, and were killed and wounded along with the soldiers. That was hard enough for Americans to comprehend. Then at the bitter campaign's end, the Americans, who had lost 3,500, saw a sight that truly strained their credulity. "There, on the northernmost point of Saipan," said correspondent Robert Sherrod, "a large segment of the Japanese civilian population was calmly, deliberately committing suicide." They were walking into the sea.

The only living human among hundreds of corpses in one Saipan cave, a badly hurt, fly-covered baby is lifted tenderly by an American. "Many a tough Marine," Sherrod cabled, "seeing a child who had been unavoidably wounded, murmured: 'What a hell of a thing war is!'"

Gene Smith photographed a mother and son scampering from a cave entrance masked by smoke and dust from an explosion. Smith came through Saipan and Iwo Jima (page 290) without a wound, but was badly wounded later on Okinawa by a mortar-shell fragment.

Peleliu escalates the cost

With the Marines on Peleliu, LIFE artist Tom Lea painted frightful scenes. This Marine had just landed. "Something exploded," Lea wrote.

"He scrambled up from the ground as if embarrassed. He looked at his left arm and stumbled back to the beach. He never fired a shot."

Battle fatigue hollows the eyes of a Marine at Bloody Nose Ridge. Lea recalled: "Last evening he came down out of the hills. He left the States 31 months ago. He was wounded in his first campaign. He has had tropical diseases. He gouges Japs out of holes each day. Two thirds of his company have been killed, but he is still standing. So he will return to attack this morning. How much can a human being endure?"

Island Inferno

The battles for the last two island steps to Japan, Iwo Jima and Okinawa, rank among the costliest in U.S. history. There the philosophy of noble death for the homeland coincided with the stark fact that the islands were respectively only 675 and 550 miles from Tokyo. On Okinawa, Japanese defense philosophy took the form of massive kamikaze attacks. They exacted an enormous naval toll (36 ships sunk, nearly 400 damaged, more than 700 fleet aircraft lost, 4,900 sailors killed or missing and 4,800 wounded) and contributed heavily to U.S. land casualties (7,600 killed, 31,700 wounded). On Iwo Jima, a volcanic ash pile honeycombed with caves, tunnels and pillboxes, the resistance manifested itself in a form already familiar to the U.S. island hoppers.

Iwo's eight square miles, over which the Marines finally raised the Stars and Stripes, was for a hellish month one of the most densely populated areas on earth, with 10,000 battling men to the square mile. It was also, said Marine commander Lieutenant General Holland Smith, the costliest territory in the Corp's 168 years, tougher than Tarawa, Kwajalein or Saipan. Only one other U.S. offensive action, Pickett's Civil War charge at Gettysburg, had so great a percentage of casualties. On Iwo's scrub-dotted lower plateau and on Mount Suribachi, the barren, sulfur-steaming volcano that rises above it, 6,800 Marines were killed and more than 18,200 wounded. The Japanese left more than 20,000 dead. Admiral Chester Nimitz's final communiqué of the battle could have served as a joint statement for both forces: on Iwo Jima, "Uncommon valor was a common virtue."

In a photograph by A.P.'s Joe Rosenthal, which has become as famous as the battle was historic, Marines raise the flag atop Mount Suribachi.

Amid the burned-out remains of a banyan jungle, Marines blow up a cave that hid a blockhouse and Japanese who refused to leave.

Iwo Jima's suicidal defense turns it into an ashy lunar landscape

On an Iwo Jima ridge, black and desolate with old volcanic ash from Mount Suribachi, U.S. Marines crouch in foxholes, seeking cover

from Japanese mortars and rocket shells. Beside them lie bodies of friends and foes, some of them half-buried in the shifting ash. All the way up the treeless ridge the Marines were exposed to the fire of batteries that could not be stilled, even with constant pounding by naval guns including the 16-inchers of six battleships. "It was sickening," correspondent Robert Sherrod wired, "to watch the Jap mortars crash into the men as they climbed. They died with the greatest possible violence. Nowhere in the Pacific war have I seen such badly mangled bodies."

Twilight for Tojo

With B-29s operating from the Marianas, Tokyo received ever-greater punishment. But the results were not proportionate to the cost in planes, crews and airbase manpower. Then, a few weeks before the invasion of Okinawa, Marianas bomber chief General Curtis E. LeMay switched from high-altitude daylight bombing to low-level night attacks with incendiaries. In one three-hour strike on March 9, 300 B-29s hit a densely populated part of Tokyo. They destroyed approximately one fourth of the city's flammable buildings, leveled more than 15 square miles, killed more than 83,000 and wounded 40,000.

LeMay gave Nagoya, Osaka, Kobe and Yokohama the same treatment, almost completely destroying them. Once Okinawa was available as a base, his XXI Bomber Command and Halsey's Third Fleet stepped up their bombing of Tokyo and blasted the remainder of the Japanese fleet out of the water. When George Silk was able to fly over Tokyo after V-J Day, only some 380,000 buildings out of nearly 1.4 million were still standing. Only two cities, Hiroshima and Nagasaki, had been more thoroughly razed—though they had witnessed an epochal new kind of bombing. The destruction spelled a defeat so total that Japan's premier was impelled to attempt suicide *(opposite)*.

◀ Shattered by U.S. bombers, the *Hyuga*, a 32,000-ton battleship with a staging deck aft for catapult planes, settles at her mooring at Kure.

A scattering of the most permanent concrete and steel structures dots a flattened industrial section of Tokyo along the Sumida River at war's end.

Because the bombs had been incendiary instead of high-explosive, highways and bridges were still passable—but traffic was nonexistent.

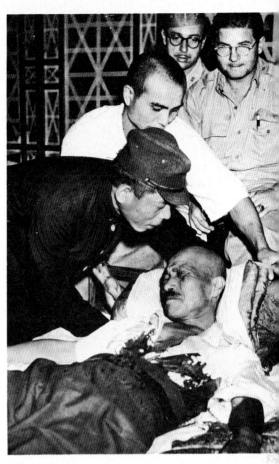

Bleeding Premier Hideki Tojo winces with pain after trying to put a bullet through his heart. He lived to be hanged as a war criminal.

Ostracized by his fellow officers in ▶ the Omori prison camp for his failure in war and suicide, Tojo reads while awaiting his war-crimes trial.

Atom-age President

Fireball: a Frightful War's Frightful End

Ironically, the seeds of America's ultimate victory over Japan were sown in the basement of Columbia University's Pupin Physics laboratories in 1939, before World War II had begun. There scientists had succeeded in splitting uranium atoms, with the possible consequent release of unimaginably large amounts of energy. Other nations, including Germany (as LIFE pointed out at the time), had access to the same information. But it was only when German refugee Albert Einstein, at the prodding of concerned fellow scientists, pointed out the military implications of nuclear fission to F.D.R. that something was done about it.

An advisory committee on uranium was set up, which led to the eventual launching in 1942 of the $2 billion Manhattan Project. Its goal was to use in a bomb fissionable material with 40 million times the power of TNT. When Japan turned down a demand for unconditional surrender, President Harry S Truman on August 6, 1945, ordered an atom bomb dropped on Hiroshima. Sixty-six thousand people were killed. A second bomb was exploded at Nagasaki on August 9 and 39,000 Japanese died. Five days later World War II was over.

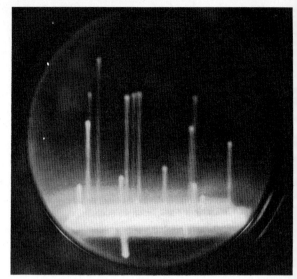

"In 50 years the picture above will probably be among the most famous in the archives of science," LIFE marveled in 1939 of Fritz Goro's photograph of the effects of splitting a uranium atom. "A new age of power is 50 years away or just around the corner," the editors added cryptically. The story was buried in the middle of the April 24 issue—it was not even listed in the table of contents—and went virtually unnoticed by the public. Unknown to LIFE (and almost everyone else not in on the secret), the "new age of power" was only six years away.

◀A radioactive mushroom-shaped cloud rises 30,000 feet over Nagasaki after a B-29 flying from the captured Japanese island of Tinian dropped its A-bomb over the industrial city.

The power of the atomic bomb that struck Hiroshima, equivalent to 20,000 tons of TNT, flung this bus across the devastated city.

Stunned and bewildered Japanese file through the wasteland that had once been Nagasaki. Taken by Yosuke Yamahata, a Japanese Army photographer, this picture and others of atomic-bomb damage were suppressed by jittery U.S. military censors until the end of the Occupation in 1952. What the pictures could not show were the side effects of the plutonium bomb—radiation poisoning that would turn many survivors of the initial blast into progressive invalids who suffered loss of hair, bleeding gums, and debilitation until they died weeks, months, even years later.

The hands of this watch, frozen at 8:16, pinpoint the moment its wearer died in the searing heat of the atomic bomb that destroyed Hiroshima.

Sober rites and a wild New York kiss ring down the curtain

Japan's Foreign Minister Mamoru Shigemitsu and Imperial Army General Yoshijiro Umezu wait to sign surrender documents aboard the *Missouri*. Shigemitsu leans on his cane to support an artificial leg that replaced a limb lost when a bomb was thrown at him in Shanghai. A sailor in Manhattan's Times Square celebrates Japan's surrender by planting a vigorous kiss on the lips of an Army nurse, a stranger until then. Alfred Eisenstaedt's picture ▶ symbolized the demonstrations—of relief and joy—that went on all over America at the end of World War II.

INDEX

Numerals in italics indicate an illustration of the subject mentioned.

PICTURE CREDITS
Credits from left to right are separated by semicolons, from top to bottom by dashes.

I. 8 Harris & Ewing; Margaret Bourke-White, LPS (2)—Leon Daniel; Ellen Auerbach; Carl Mydans, LPS—BS; Peter Stackpole, LPS; Margaret Bourke-White, LPS—Torkel Korling; Robert Capa, LPS; Frank Scherschel. 10 Pix—Robert Capa, BS. 11 PI. 12,13 Joris Ivens, director/John Ferno, photographer. 14 Robert Capa, Magnum; Robert Capa, LPS—Three Lions. 15. Robert Capa, LPS. 16,17 Younosuke Natori, INT—INT—WW; PI. 18,19 Tsuguichi Koyanagi; Paul Dorsey. 20 A. T. Steele—WW—Robert Capa, LPS; March of Time. 21 Edgar Snow (2)—Bosshard, BS—Bosshard, BS. 22,23 Ferd Vogel—Wolfgang Weber—Alfred Eisenstaedt, LPS; Hugo Jaeger. 24 DePascal, PI (2)—DePascal, PI; INT; Keystone—Lilo Maier, PI; WW. 25 INT; Interphoto—WW. 26,27 No credit; PI. 28 INT; European; WW—INT; WW—PI; European (2). 29 Hugo Jaeger. 30,31 Margaret Bourke-White, LPS—no credit; Schall, Pix; Keystone. 32 Ellen Auerbach—Fritz Goro; Illustration reproduced by permission of and © by Brown & Bigelow, St. Paul, Minnesota. 33 Dmitri Kessel; Frank Scherschel—Fritz Henle, BS. 34 European—Otto Hagel. 35 Otto Hagel. 36,37 WW; War Department—Acme—WW; War Department. 38 Margaret Bourke-White, LPS; Magee, PI—Pacific Press Service; WW. 39 PI—March of Time. 40,41 WW; WW; Acme—PI—PI; WW. 42 John Phillips, LPS—INT; PI. 43 European. 44 Sovfoto. 45 Dever, BS—WW. 46 Dever, BS. 47 PI.

II. 48 No credit; Hans Groenhoff; British Combine—John Phillips, LPS; David E. Scherman, LPS; W. Eugene Smith, BS—W. Eugene Smith, BS; Robert Yarnell Richie; W. Eugene Smith, BS—William Vandivert, LPS; Charles Brown; Gabriel Benzur—Margaret Bourke-White, LPS; Walter B. Lane; WW. 50,51 Alfred Eisenstaedt, LPS—Acme; Official U.S. Army Photo. 52 United Israel Appeal—Jack Powell—Jack Powell. 53 Dever, BS. 54 Acme—Acme; WW; WW—David E. Scherman, LPS; Acme; Walter Sanders, BS. 55 INT; David E. Scherman, LPS—George Strock; Acme—Martin Harris; WW; Keith Dennison, Oakland Tribune. 56,57 INT—INT; David Ritchie, PI (2); Carl Mydans, LPS; Illustrated. 58 Sted Jones; map by Anthony Sodaro—Paris-Match. 59 Paris-Match. 60,61 Carl Mydans, LPS; Triangle Photo—Carl Mydans, LPS; Triangle Photo—Triangle Photo. 62,63 Dever, BS—Interphoto; European. 64 Margaret Bourke-White, LPS; no credit—Fox Photos; Radio Times Hulton Picture Library—Stephen Cribb; Jarché, PI. 65 PI; no credit; no credit—PI—PI; British Official Photo. 66 Margaret Bourke-White, LPS; Interphoto—Interphoto. 67 Interphoto. 68,69 WW—Fox Photos; PI (2) 70,71 PI (5)—INT; Movietone News. 72,73 WW—John Topham, BS; INT. 74,75 Cecil Beaton, PI; London Daily Mirror, PI; William Vandivert, LPS—posters by Walter Lane (2); Dorothy Diamond, PI. 76 William Vandivert, LPS. 77 PI. 78 Harris & Ewing. 79 British Combine—PI; British Combine—WW; PI. 80 British Combine—David E. Scherman, LPS; London Daily Mirror. 81 WW. 82 Underwood & Underwood—no credit. 83 WW. 84 Bob Landry, LPS—Eliot Elisofon, LPS—diagram by B. G. Seielstad. 85 Eliot Elisofon, LPS. 86,87 George Strock, LPS; Thomas D. McAvoy, LPS. 88 Private Stewart L. Elliott. 89 John Phillips. 90 British Combine—Pictorial Press, BS; David E. Scherman, LPS—David E. Scherman, LPS. 91 INT. 92 Dever, BS. 93 London Daily Mirror. 94,95 No credit. 96,97 WW; map by Anthony Sodaro and Frank Stockman—Acme; Dever, BS (2). 98 Margaret Bourke-White, LPS—British Official Photo. 99 INT. 100,101 British Official Photo; Otto Hagel—Margaret Bourke-White, LPS. 102 Acme—WW; Walter Sanders, BS. 103 John Phillips. 104 Mainichi Shimbun, Acme. 105 Thomas D. McAvoy, LPS.

III. 106 Dmitri Kessel, LPS; George Strock, LPS; Hans Groenhoff—William C. Shrout, LPS; J. R. Eyerman, LPS; Dmitri Kessel, LPS—George Strock, LPS; William C. Shrout, LPS; J. R. Eyerman, LPS—Nina Leen; J. R. Eyerman, LPS; Myron Davis, LPS—Dmitri Kessel, LPS; Gjon Mili, LPS; Bob Landry, LPS. 108,109 George A. Douglas—Charles W. Miller Studio; U.S. Navy Photo. 110 George Strock, LPS. 111 Gordon Coster, LPS—William C. Shrout, LPS. 112,113 Stanfield & Staab, Milwaukee Journal; Ralph Amdursky. 114,115 Carl Mydans, LPS; map by Anthony Sodaro and Frank Stockman—Carl Mydans, LPS; drawing by Alexander Leydenfrost. 116 Melville Jacoby—Melville Jacoby; no credit. 117 INT—drawing by Fred Wren. 118 U.S. Navy Photo, WW—Ralph Morse, LPS—U.S.A.A.F. Photo, INT. 119 WW. 120,121 U.S. Navy Photo—map by Anthony Sodaro and Frank Stockman—U.S. Navy Photo; model by Norman Bel Geddes. 122 Frank Scherschel, LPS. 123 U.S. Navy Photo—Jack Wilkes, LPS. 124 Eliot Elisofon, LPS. 125 Cartoon by Edmund Duffy, Baltimore Sun—Carl Mydans, LPS—Domonken, BS; INT. 126 Posters by Koehler & Ancona; D. Bryers—M. Klein; X. Gonzales; Sergeant J. Dumas. 127 Posters by A. Brotman; H. Melzian—W. Pursell—J. Willard; G. V. Lewis; O. Nelson. 128,129 George Strock, LPS—George Silk, LPS; George Strock, LPS (3). 130,131 George Strock, LPS. 132 Nelson Morris—Ralph Morse, LPS; U.S. Marine Corps Photo. 133 Ralph Morse, LPS—map by Michael Phillips; Ralph Morse, LPS. 134,135 Painting by Tom Lea. 136 Alfred Eisenstaedt, LPS—U.S. Marine Corps Photo. 137 Ralph Morse, LPS. 138 John Phillips—Frank Scherschel, LPS; Ralph Morse, LPS—Walter Sanders (3). 139 Ralph Crane, BS. 140,141 Herbert Gehr, LPS; Myron Davis, LPS; Eliot Elisofon, LPS; Margaret Bourke-White, LPS; J. R. Eyerman, LPS; Martin Munkacsi; Alfred Eisenstaedt, LPS; Peter Stackpole, LPS—Margaret Bourke-White, LPS; Marie Hansen, LPS; Peter Stackpole, LPS—Peter Stackpole, LPS. 142 Dmitri Kessel, LPS; Walter Sanders, LPS—Bud Fraker, Paramount; WW. 143 Carol Eyerman. 144 K. Chester. 145 Charles E. Steinheimer, LPS—Charles E. Steinheimer, LPS; Ralph Morse, LPS. 146,147 British Official Photo—George Rodger, LPS; British Official Photo; INT—British Official Photo; INT. 148,149 Painting by Fletcher Martin; Eliot Elisofon, LPS—Hart Preston, LPS; painting by Fletcher Martin. 150 Map by Anthony Sodaro and Frank Stockman—Eliot Elisofon, LPS. 151 WW—Eliot Elisofon, LPS; British Official Photo. 152 Philippe Halsman; Martha Holmes, LPS—Nina Leen; Andreas Feininger, LPS. 153 Peter Stackpole, LPS; Nina Leen; Eliot Elisofon, LPS—Walter Sanders, BS. 154 Ralph Vincent, Portland Journal. 155. Eric Schaal, LPS—Nelson Morris (2)—R. E. Stackard; Eric Schaal, LPS. 158,159 Frank Scherschel, LPS—Eliot Elisofon, LPS—Frank Scherschel, LPS—Fritz Goro, LPS; painting by Anton O. Fischer. 160 Frank Scherschel, LPS. 161 Dmitri Kessel, LPS. 162 Roman Vishniac, BS—Leo Rosenthal (2). 163 Pix. 164,165 Sovfoto—Margaret Bourke-White, LPS—INT; Sovfoto. 166,167 INT; U.S.S.R. Official Photo—INT—INT; Acme.

IV. 168 U.S. Army Signal Corps Photo; Frank Scherschel, LPS; Peter Stackpole, LPS—Eliot Elisofon, LPS; Sam Levitz, Arizona Daily Star; Eliot Elisofon, LPS—Paul Dorsey; Dmitri Kessel, LPS (2)—Walter Sanders, LPS; Gordon Coster; Eliot Elisofon, LPS—Eileen Darby, Graphic House; Nina Leen; David E. Scherman, LPS. 170,171 William C. Shrout, LPS—painting by David Fredenthal. 172,173 U.S. 8th A.F. Photo; INT—Myron Davis, LPS. 174 U.S. Marine Corps Photo—U.S. Marine Corps Photo, Acme. 175 U.S. Marine Corps Photo, WW—WW. 176,177 George Strock, LPS. 178 John Florea, LPS (2)—George Karger, LPS. 179 WW—Ralph Crane, BS. 180 George Silk, LPS. 181 Frank Scherschel, LPS; Charles Cort, Acme; Gene Lester—George Karger, LPS. 182,183 PI; Margaret Bourke-White, LPS—Eliot Elisofon, LPS; Margaret Bourke-White, LPS; British Combine—David E. Scherman, LPS; Frank Scherschel, LPS—William C. Shrout, LPS; U.S.A.A.F. Photo. 184 U.S.A.A.F. Photo, INT—U.S. 8th A.F. Fighter Command Photos (3). 185 British Official Photo; U.S.A.A.F. Photo—U.S. 8th A.F. Fighter Command Photos (2)—Frank Scherschel, LPS. 186,187 Drawing by Alexander Leydenfrost. 188 Eric Schaal, LPS—Thomas D. McAvoy, LPS; Alfred Eisenstaedt, LPS. 189 Alfred Eisenstaedt, LPS (2)—Alfred Eisenstaedt, LPS; Edward Clark, LPS. 190,191 Edmund B. Gerard. 192,193 Andreas Feininger, LPS (2)—Boeing Aircraft. 194 New York Daily News. 195 WW. 196,197 Alfred Eisenstaedt, LPS. 198,199 WW; Dmitri Kessel, LPS—Acme (2); Dmitri Kessel, LPS. 200,201 Bob Landry, LPS; Ewing Krainin; 20th Century Fox—Bob Landry, LPS. 202,203 George Rodger, INT (2)—Thomas Kwang, Paul Guillumette—George Rodger—George Rodger; University of California Library, Berkeley. 204,205 U.S. Army Photo; William Vandivert, LPS. 206 Map by Anthony Sodaro and Frank Stockman—William Vandivert, LPS; Bernard Hoffman, LPS. 207 Bernard Hoffman, LPS. 208 Eliot Elisofon, LPS—Jack Wilkes, LPS. 209 James Thomas, The Cleveland Press; Stephen N. Lemanis; Alfred Eisenstaedt, LPS—Harold Trudeau; Peter Stackpole, LPS; Harold Trudeau—Hansel Mieth and Otto Hagel, LPS; Ralph Crane, BS; William Vandivert, LPS. 210 Kosti Ruohomaa, BS; PI—Otto Hagel, LPS. 211 WW. 212,213 George Rodger, LPS—Bob Landry, LPS; model by Norman Bel Geddes. 214,215 Robert Capa, LPS. 216 U.S. Signal Corps Photo—drawing by Alexander Leydenfrost—Sandro Aurisiccio de Val. 217 Robert Capa, LPS. 218,219 U.S. Signal Corps Photo. 220,221 Robert Capa, LPS—George Silk, LPS (2). 222 George Silk, LPS. 223 Tony Griffin, WW—Office of Strategic Services. 224,225 John Phillips, LPS; paintings by Bernard Perlin. 226 From the MGM release A GUY NAMED JOE © 1944 Loew's. Copyright renewed 1971 by Metro-Goldwyn-Mayer; Longworth, Warner Brothers—Peter Stackpole, LPS; Two Cities Films. 227 James F. Laughead—From the MGM release HOMECOMING © 1948 Loew's. Copyright renewed 1975 by Metro-Goldwyn-Mayer; Bob Landry, LPS. 228 William Wallace, United Artists—Loomis Dean, LPS; Universal. 229 Universal, Culver Pictures—Universal. 230 © 1977 by Milton Caniff—© 1977 by Milton Caniff—© Bill Mauldin. 231 George Baker; © Bill Mauldin; Lieutenant Dave Breger—George Baker—Lieutenant Dave Breger. 232,233 Painting by Floyd Davis—David E. Scherman, LPS (3). 234,235 Frank Scherschel, LPS—WW; Frank Scherschel, LPS.

V. 236 Lockheed Photo by Erik Miller; David E. Scherman, LPS; William C. Shrout, LPS—Thomas D. McAvoy, LPS; John Florea, LPS; Gregory Weil—W. Eugene Smith, LPS; William Vandivert, LPS; William C. Shrout, LPS—U.S. Navy Photo; © Karsh, Ottawa; Peter Stackpole, LPS—Dmitri Kessel, LPS; Eliot Elisofon, LPS; © Karsh, Ottawa from British Combine. 238,239 U.S. Army Photo; Robert Capa, LPS—Bob Landry, LPS—U.S. Coast Guard Photo; Robert Capa, LPS. 240,241 Frank Scherschel, LPS; Bob Landry, LPS—map by Anthony Sodaro and Frank Stockman; Frank Scherschel, LPS (2). 242,243 Paintings by Aaron Bohrod (2)—Ogden Pleissner (2). 244,245 Leonard McCombe, LPS. 246 © Arnold Newman; map by Raphael Palacios—George Silk, LPS—INT; Bert Brandt, Acme. 247 Horace Cort, WW. 248,249 Frank Scherschel, LPS—Frank Scherschel, LPS; Ralph Morse, LPS (2). 250,251 Painting by Floyd Davis. 252,253 Bob Landry, LPS—David E. Scherman, LPS; Robert Capa, LPS. 254 Harold Trudeau; Gordon Coster—Eric Schaal, LPS; Alfred Eisenstaedt, LPS—Acme; Kosti Ruohomaa, BS (2). 255 WW; Dave Dornberg, Acme—Acme—© 1938 by Williamson Music Inc.; George Karger, LPS; Universal—Kosti Ruohomaa; U.S. Army Photo, INT; Thomas D. McAvoy, LPS. 256 David E. Scherman, LPS—U.S. Army Signal Corps Photo. 257 John Florea, LPS. 258,259 George Silk, LPS. 260,261 Ralph Morse, LPS. 262 Drawings by Matt Greene (2); Hans Wild, LPS. 263 George Rodger, LPS. 264 Ralph Morse, LPS—U.S. Signal Corps Photo, Acme—map by Anthony Sodaro and Frank Stockman. 265 John Florea, LPS. 266 George Silk, LPS; map by Rafael Palacios—George Silk, LPS (2)—George Silk, LPS (2). 267 George Silk, LPS. 268 George Silk, LPS. 269 Robert Capa, LPS. 270,271 WW; U.S. Army Signal Corps Photo—Thomas D. McAvoy, LPS; WW (2); Edward Clark, LPS. 272 PI—N. Petrova—Preslit, Sovfoto. 273 U.S. Army Signal Corps Photo. 274,275 Robert Capa, LPS (4)—Ralph Morse, LPS—U.S. Army Signal Corps Photo, WW (2). 276 Margaret Bourke-White, LPS—George Rodger, LPS. 277 Margaret Bourke-White, LPS—George Rodger, LPS; William Vandivert, LPS. 278 William Vandivert, LPS—Leonard McCombe, LPS. 279 Margaret Bourke-White, LPS; no credit—John Florea, LPS; Leonard McCombe, LPS. 280 Eileen Darby, Graphic House—Martha Holmes, LPS. 281 Sam Shere, LPS. 282 U.S. Coast Guard Photo, WW. 283 Irving Haberman, PM Photo. 284,285 Andrew Lopez, Acme—Carl Mydans, LPS; Frank Prist, Acme—Werner, Chicago Sun; Mark Kauffman; WW. 286,287 W. Eugene Smith, LPS. 288,289 Paintings by Tom Lea. 290,291 Joe Rosenthal, WW; W. Eugene Smith, LPS. 292,293 Joe Rosenthal, WW. 294,295 U.S. Navy Photo; George Silk, LPS; Charles Gory, WW—George Silk, LPS. 296 © Karsh, Ottawa; Fritz Goro—3rd Photo Squadron, 20th U.S.A.A.F. 297 Bernard Hoffman, LPS. 298,299 Yosuke Yamahata from "Atom Bombed Nagasaki," Daiichi Shuppan-Sha, Tokyo; Brian Brake, Magnum. 300 Carl Mydans, LPS. 301 Alfred Eisenstaedt, LPS.

Abbreviations: ©, copyright; BS, Black Star; INT, International News Photo; LPS, Life Picture Service; PI, Pictures Inc.; WW, Wide World